MARELLA is a fashion designer b' adoption.

In her adolescence she enc which lit her passion for literature, reading and writing, complementing the artistic skills which she nurtured ever since she was a child, particularly in the areas of drawing and garment design. This blend of experiences led her to undergo college studies in Design & Fashion Technologies, which she graduated in in 2015, and to continue in the following years by pursuing higher studies at the Central Saint Martins School, in London, UK, while in parallel nurturing her continuous learning desire through several focused courses.

Throughout her studies, Marella achieved numerous Fashion Awards and Recognitions and, in parallel to that, she also took her first steps in the professional world by working at a number of renowned brands such as Krizia and Marni, amongst the others.

Her passion for writing took an unexpected turn into a career through a fortuitous meeting with emeritus Prof. Ruth Finnegan, who gave her the opportunity to explore aspects related to the creative process. This meeting opened the doors for Marella to deepen her involvement in socio-anthropological issues such as women condition, individual sexuality, the contradictions of our contemporary era, etc. all of which she is particularly engaged in, both online and physically.

Born in Bari, on the South-East coast of Italy, she spent part of her early years across different Italian cities and finally moved to Central London in 2016, where she is currently based, despite her love for travel which keeps carrying her around the globe.

FROM BLANK CANVAS TO GARMENT

A Creative Journey of Discovery

MARELLA CAMPAGNA

BALESTIER PRESS
LONDON · SINGAPORE

Balestier Press
71-75 Shelton Street, London WC2H 9JQ
www.balestier.com

From Blank Canvas to Garment:
A Creative Journey of Discovery
Copyright © Marella Campagna, 2019

First published by Balestier Press in 2019

A CIP catalogue record for this book
is available from the British Library.

ISBN 978 1 911221 66 1

to my mother and my father

Contents

Preface

Curiosity is the base of every creative process.
Curiosity taught me everything I know about fashion, the world in general, and actually it still drives my learning process.

It has given me the willingness of pushing my boundaries both in the creative fields and with myself.

I am a very curious person, after all.

I have always shown a particular interest in the environment around me, objects, nature, people's mind and thoughts, capabilities, and reactions with the purpose of learning more, discover different realities and options. This approach has helped me to better understand my ego, passions and aims while enjoying this amazing journey through our lives, collecting pieces, stories and inspirations everywhere.

I know, it might sound weird, and you would wonder how it is possible to deepen yourself when you are focused on others.

This is, in my opinion, the magical power of curiosity.

When you are eager to learn, you allow things to go and flow freely inside your mind, enriching yourself in a way and developing a better sense of awareness about the surroundings and a more conscious approach concerning your inner personality, tastes, potential.

"Ideas always come from other ideas" my tutor once said, and this is all about the importance of being open, sharing, and investigating.

He used to encourage us to be inquisitive and keen to explore several subjects and topics, because studying provides you with a strong knowledge and background to build on something new.

The more you search, the more you are going to face questions and doubts, evaluating and examining different things, unconsciously pushing yourself a bit further compared to your starting point.

This approach might be slightly scary at the beginning, but scary things lead you out of your comfort zone, which is crucial for the growth of an individual.

In my case this critical process offered me a guideline to follow and to let my work progress into the right direction.

So do not be afraid of opening up your eyes and minds to the world, ask, share, learn, you are not going to lose your identity in this multitude of information and realities, you will have the possibility to expand your personal world of experiences, generating new ideas.

It is essential to realise that it will be our ability to learn, unlearn, relearn, re-evaluate and change, that will hold the key to all our "creative futures".

CHAPTER ONE

Beginning

I used to be a terrible child, curious and terrible.

My parents were proud of me in a way, but, honestly speaking, pretty exhausted.

I started my "personal investigation", cutting off all my Barbies' hair, painting their faces with messy and colourful make up.

At some point I also decided to build them a proper apartment, made of cardboards and fabrics, but unfortunately this did not lead me into an interior designer career, on the contrary it helped me reflecting on how relevant and essential was shaping and creating surreal worlds, while taking care of all the details and things involved.

Playing in these kind of meta-realities is very common among children, it is a key moment of the creativity growth and discovery process, so that, in my case, the very crucial thing went beyond the play itself.

Make up, haircuts and garments were my childish vehicles to communicate and talk about something, every Barbie had a specific role reinforced by the "outfit", there was already a kind of connection between clothes and concepts, although they all looked like clowns at the time.

Visual things became my mean of communication, a method to explore my personality, feelings and thoughts.

Luckily for my parents, who stopped buying me dolls (considering that I ruined them all), I moved to fabrics and paper, as a proper beginning of my journey.

There was a moment in the year, probably a couple of months before summertime, during which my grandmother used to come and visit us for some days (she said, actually ending up in a month or two).

She was an example to me, I considered her as an artist, she could paint, play piano, sew, embroider, draw and so on, and she used to carry in her luggage tonnes of exciting little things which made me crave a lot.

Her bags contained a whole world, there were items for every type of needs, and I could not wait for the moment she had opened one of them, revealing some new treasures to play with.

We used to spend days and nights, together, working on different "projects" and discussing books and photos, me sitting on her bed scribbling somewhere, her, sewing some clothes with those long and delicate fingers.

I loved to interrupt her with unlikely questions to see a "gently disappointed face" and ear her tone turning into a kind of serious one, her voice was so warm and vibrant.

One day, she gave me this consumed pencil and softly invited me:

"Marella, do you fancy drawing something this time, so we can then work together on your idea?"

She wanted me to conduct the play, to be honest I did not know what to do, and, most importantly, I totally ignored I had any ability to do that.

Calling the shots was, generally, her job, she acted as a "creative director", giving a brief, concepts and tasks, and well, I was an intern.

I looked into her friendly eyes and then at the white piece

FROM BLANK CANVAS TO GARMENT

of paper just in front of me, realizing that I was having my "first empty canvas crisis syndrome".

Thousands of thoughts passed through my mind, there was a thing that unsettled me, I was worrying about MY performance, my OWN evaluation.

My aim was to show myself first, and then my grandmother (generally very supportive with me) I could live up to the work, but, as all of you can imagine, the more we care about our performance, the more we are likely to jeopardise it.

It is quite common to notice that the fiercest judge of an individual's performance is the person itself, thus, most of us grew up by absorbing the idea of failure as something inevitably affecting our sense of confidence, rather than as a vehicle of knowledge gathering and improvement.

This is why when we are asked to show our capabilities, we tend to feel lost, doubtful and paralysed, instead of just being excited.

In my opinion this is the real big misconception behind the idea of "failure".

The possibility of failing is often conceived as a completely disruptive and negative situation, that talented and intelligent individuals never face in their lives (luckily a quite surreal perspective), so that enabling yourself to accept it would subconsciously mean being less gifted.

Therefore, it is quite obvious that the hypothesis of a crash could be, for most of us, terribly scary.

According to this deep-rooted fear of failing, at that time I unconsciously did not allow myself to try, trapping a multitude of useful ideas.

I was stuck, kept on repeating that I should have not

embarrassed myself.

Instead, what I was really forgetting is that missing an opportunity in order to avoid mistakes, is not a wise decision, failure represents an essential part of the learning process, to put ourselves to test and develop a critical approach, with the purpose of constantly improving our skills.

Meanwhile, the white sheet was still waiting for me, so I decided to grab that pencil, giving myself a chance.

I squeezed it hard with my fingers, squinting and searching for something interesting

and inspiring in the room, yet I was actually peering into my head.

My concern was where to find inspiration when stuck and scared.

"Oh well" I thought "Maybe I can find it among the things I love, they can turn my creativity on, they can guide me when I feel lost, it is so natural, after all".

So I did, I drew a garment.

It was a dress, with a very basic bodice and a pleated skirt, taken from the world of Japanese Mangas (I was so into it at that time).

Volumes and proportions were not that real, and even if my draft looked a bit weird, made my heart quiver.

My grandmother seemed really excited to see it, finding it nice and interesting (the way only grandmothers, positive and supportive, could be).

Once decided the fit and finishings such as where to allocate zip, seams and pleats, we moved to the next step, creating a proper paper pattern.

I have never imagined a garment could be that technical.

I had been always considering arty works as a kind of escape route from the terrible, boring school subjects like maths and so on, but I was terribly wrong.

Concerning the "making of" a pattern, design process and fabric sourcing a part, everything is about numbers and mathematical calculations, in order to create a wearable shape perfectly fitted on a body.

"So, Marella" my grandmother suggested with her calm voice "Clothes have to fit the person, never the contrary, and according to this fundamental principle, it is essential to consider the body size and shape, related proportions and measures, distribute the centimetres in a balanced way while sketching the pattern...." and I was already losing my train of thoughts. At a first glance it seemed terribly complicated. Then, following her practical instructions, while having the privilege to see the "genius" at work, I started with some notes, ending up with the lower part of the dress, my lovely first pleated skirt.

Skirt centre front, made of paper and secured with pins: I put some marks between every pleat as a guideline to follow, so that once opened and laid out on the fabric, it is easier to place the folds exactly as in the sample.

Once moved my first step into that exciting new reality, the necessity of unleashing my creativity and discovering my tastes grew up progressively in me.

I started to collect fabric scraps, pictures, and clothes references, sticking them into a little booklet with all the relevant notes, scribbles and garment drafts, as I had previously learnt from my grandmother.

It became my fashion daily diary, my first ever sketch-book that every artist should have.

I used to indulge in my loneliness, secretly enjoying that silent and pervasive process, completely ignoring where it would have led me.

I spent so many days, months, working on my small little world, made up of dresses, drawings and paintings, shaping my happy universe, my happy place.

It could not have lasted for a lifetime, just like childhood cannot, school was upon me and I had to move forward.

I was forced to abandon all of my beloved habits into a box, and sadly lock it.

At that time my parents were kind of headstrong and obsessed with the importance of "classical and academic studies" (undeniably essential) to understand that, in my case, the learning process was also passing through experimentation and self-discovery.

Fashion was frivolous, almost a whim, unworthy of either mine or their attention.

They did not encourage me to persist that path, suggesting, on the contrary to switch to the "real world" made of "consistent and tangible jobs".

Reasonably, it was not their fault.

They grew up in this warm little town, with a terribly

enchanting seaside and delicious food, experiencing a sense of time as being somehow suspended, everything was always the same, especially people's way of thinking, too stiff and focused on appearances.

There was a kind of static feeling in that "heavenly place", same colours, same faces, same habits, and same air, always smelling like spring.

The paradise of the unchanged.

Obviously, fashion was too progressive for that conservative reality, creative fields were not accepted as part of an individual's working life, earning on the contrary a really negative reputation.

Although art holds a prominent role within society, gaining general attention and recognition, when confronted with an artist's world, people tend to become scared and prejudicial, based on a misbelief built over the years. Arty people have always been diverse, outsiders and somehow crazy, due to their "insane, thoughtless" way of living, full of excesses and anti-social behaviours, or "lunatic appearance".

The only responsibility by these individuals for their "unacceptable approach" is trying to set up the rules into their own private space, exploring and shaping their personality rather than caring about established conventions.

Ultimately, who cares if somebody has colourful hair, and dresses like a "clown"?

Does it affect their intelligence?

Does it compromise their performance?

Yes, it did for those people at that time, and actually it did for my parents, too.

Their aim was to protect me from a hypothetical break up, but luckily all of their efforts were completely in vain, in the end.

I enrolled into classical studies, focusing in particular on humanistic subjects, but at least I was fortunate enough to nurture my passion, thanks to a course program partially centred on history of art.

During my period at high school, I had the possibility to read, search and investigate a lot, focusing on artists and authors I was passionate about, driven by my incessant curiosity and enthusiasm. I found it essential to leave a private space at the end of the day, dedicated to my aims and passions, with the purpose of secretly pursuing my pathway.

Nobody could have ever guaranteed me how easy or difficult it would have been, nor how much it would have taken, but I was determined.

Once discovered my dream, I felt I did not have any other options, despite taking into account difficulties and crashes on my way, and expecting to face potential detours.

Ultimately it is all about things "we love".

Prior to me, a number of individuals had already started as amateurs, full of doubts and fears (reasonably, as we all are), making the most of what they had, pulling out courage and dedication.[1]

It is a life-long approach, a never ending journey which will lead you to a more confident and proactive attitude, accepting your choices as a part of yourself, without over-caring about people's judgements and expectations.

In my case, managing that narrow-minded environment

---

[1]   Austin Kleon, "*Show Your Work!: 10 ways to share your creativity and get discovered*", page 37.

has been very difficult, since it resulted in a constant yet awful feeling of uncertainty and self-doubt, that constantly pushed me to look for external approval (as a legacy of my background, periodically, I still tend to replicate that pattern, when "something goes wrong with my projects").

Can you imagine what the funny part is?

Confidence never comes from the outside, and expecting a massive crowd to cheer you up is quite unrealistic.

We need to be our own supporters, and stop being ashamed of "our beloved things".

We will always love things that others might consider as "garbage", but we should find the courage to persist and celebrate them, as a distinctive mark of our own individuality, our uniqueness.

They represent the peculiarity and variety of our influences, a personal way of mixing and matching the aspects of our heritage.

So, once you find what really makes your heart beat, then you should stop caring and honour it.[2]

In the creative process, for instance, it is essential to develop and shape your own personality, so that it will influence your research and investigation methodology, with the purpose of collecting every type of stimulus, canvassing several and sometimes unusual fields, cultural leftovers, things ignored and abandoned.

A steady focus and open-minded approach will help you discover the unexpected, as "invaluable treasures are sometimes hidden behind ordinary things, that humans no longer see".[3]

---

[2]   Austin Kleon, "*Show Your Work!: 10 ways to share your creativity and get discovered*", page 89.

[3]   ibid., page 87.

According to this, after five years of traditional studies, I decided to take the risk and follow my dreams.

It was a warm afternoon, the windows were opened, a soft curtain was swaying under the restless breeze, a smooth scent of summer eased from the courtyard. It was nice and quiet. This image still makes me feel terribly emotional, of me laying on the bed waiting for my boyfriend to come, and books and comics spread all over, creating a kind of fort.

Smelling a subtle tone of the ink on the paper, dwelling on the amazing drawings, I turned the comic page and a frayed sheet fell.

My heart quivered.

It was my first ever garment drawing, it was my beloved pleated dress.

There was nobody in there, just me and that piece of paper.

Tears came to my eyes. It had been a long time, probably ten years or more, since I drew something like that, I had forced myself to move on, forgetting the poetry behind every gentle movements of my coarse pencil, even if I was tirelessly collecting inspirations and materials along the way.

I had trapped myself in the false idea that fashion would have always been a whim, nothing more.

I lied.

In that very moment I realized how much I missed it, and how much "locking that box" had costed me.

My impetus was to grab a pencil and start scribbling, again, but surprisingly my hand refused to work.

I was at point zero, where the most difficult decision within myself was whether to walk away, or to try harder.

I was full of emotions, ideas in my mind, a "beloved memory" in front waiting for me, a pencil set on it, yet even so I could not draw.

"Marella" I said "You can't do this, you are not capable anymore, time has passed, leaving behind all of your childish plays, don't waste your energy and expectations, it's no more your thing".

I was on the line, unconsciously scared; I had covered my aims so meticulously that, when in need, I could not find them.

What happened to me was nothing less than a kind of traumatic episode, in which my mind and body (in a way) as a reaction, had been adapting, in order to protect from more suffering, creating a really strong "battlement" almost insurmountable.

That battlement was my block, the reason way I was torturing me with the idea that drawing garments was no more "my thing" instead of giving myself a chance.

The battlement was my childish pain of being considered as a diverse.

But then, with the passing of the time, with my growth, memories started to melt, leaving the space, again, to my real nature.

"May the light come inside and willingness push and break that door" I thought, letting my hopes and enthusiasm enter in that peaceful afternoon.

So I did, I drew again and, unlike my expectations, I was far more able than in the past.

That day my life changed, completely.

I left economical studies (almost begun), my home town, my excuses, insecure feelings, derisions and so on, preparing myself to move to another city and finally start my BA in Fashion.

It had been so hard, but it was all worth it.

CHAPTER TWO

Moving into Fashion

First day at University.
A massive room full of sewing machines was standing up in front of me, I was already looking forward to entering and touching all of the amazing tools provided.

It was a kind of paradise, with posters of vintage Vogue stuck on the wall, drawings, piles of fabrics, huge desks...I felt terribly excited.

"Please kill me now" I thought "I want to stay here for the rest of my life".

We were a big group of students that day, colourful, unconventional and definitely chatty, I was already making new friends when a peremptory voice thundered:

"Guys, keep silent please, let me introduce my role here, I will be your industrial designer and pattern cutting tutor, and from today on you need to say goodbye to your private life. As fashion students, you are supposed to constantly produce ideas on demand, sewing, experimenting and working on different projects at a time, as quickly as possible, maintaining high levels of performance. Fashion is a fast paced environment, it is essential for you to learn how to keep up with it!"

"Oh cool" I said, after the initial thrill "We are all screwed up!"

Turning my head all around, I saw desperate and scared expressions, on my classmates' faces, I could easily imagine that we were all wondering what she was really talking about and probably reflecting on her pretty unusual and very straight to the point approach.

After all, that was what fashion is all about, going straight to the point, consistent and constant experimentations, making decisions, exploring modernity while always being focus oriented, and stay productive.

At 10 a.m. our scheduled lessons started, without a proper warm up, we had hand-drawing first, fashion drawings, fabrics and materials and industrial design.

"It couldn't have started any better", I thought.

I was delighted to see that "drawing" was finally considered as a decent and normal academic subject.

As a self-taught arty girl, I had spent my entire life with the utopian belief that creative skills belonged to some form of individual talent, something innate, without any compromises. I had never considered the possibility of structuring your own creative learning, improving your existing skills and developing new techniques.

So that, after less than one hour of hand-drawing, I experienced a kind of crash noticing my classmates performances, at a really high level, and me, well, I was the weirdo even there: disoriented, a bit frustrated, but at least free.

Days and months were passing so fast while doing a pattern, cutting a garment and studying some theory.

At that time I was obsessed with scouture and shape construction, I used to search for architectural references and designers creations, copying and printing the most inspiring pages from the school magazine archive.

My favourite designer were Rei Kawakubo, head and

"Comme des garçons" Paris Fashion show: These silhouettes still drive me crazy, even if my main focus moved from an aesthetic approach to a more technical and conceptual perspective. The impressive dimension and the bright and patent leather colour are definitely a catalyst for emotion, especially for me in the very beginning of my journey. "The bigger the garment, the better" was my mantra, as a kind of celebration of the clothes, a way of breaking the rules and let the creativity shout out loud. Rei Kawakubo is still one of my favourite designer, an unquestionable genius, her "sculptures" speak about ideas, purposes, concepts rather than "fashion". The poetry behind, to me, is represented by the use of clothes as an art form, a vehicle, making the rules instead of just sticking to trends and seasonal "must have", creating something really astonishing for people who want to reflect, endorse the same aesthetic, dream, not merely adorn their bodies. Not only this, but also her talent to perfectly combine techniques, constructions, proportion and colours, ending with very sophisticated and impressive garments, never too heavy or bulky, just spectacular.

founder of the Japanese fashion label Comme des garçons, and Iris van Erpen, owner of the eponymous brand.

I clearly remember when I had this insane idea of experimenting with big volumes and huge proportions, it was during my second year in occasion of a fashion competition launched by both mine and five other Universities.

Designers were expected to create two looks, related to and inspired by the cinematographic world.

I could have not finished my application form yet, that I was already dreaming about the prize, dwelling on the image of me walking through the catwalk with my two models.

I have always been like this, a romantic soul, so romantic that instead of focusing on the tasks I was prone to waste all of my time indulging in the happy-ending. No way!

I was too excited and determined to accomplish my goal, that when it came to make a plan and start the research process I faced the "Second blank canvas crisis" probably closer to proper "Performance anxiety".

I felt completely out of my comfort zone, having no idea about what and where to search for. I personally hated movies: not only did I detest them, but, I can now confidently say, that "I reached the highest peak of ignorance in the field".

I was tragically desperate, kept on saying things like "Oh my god, Marella, what can you do? You are not going to win anything," and the likes. It was the biggest fashion drama of my life, thus far.

After a week, being exhausted by my own pointless and disruptive approach, I decided to "get this work done", starting from a list of film makers I was interested in, writing down all possible notes related to directors' creative choices, garments style, colour palette and so on, trying to keep an eye on the themes as well.

Having watched hundreds of movies, "making of" and "behind the scenes", full of information and inputs, I finally hung out my white flag, without really understanding why all of my efforts were not worth it.

They simply did not trigger any decision, cinema had never ever meant anything to me, possibly also as a result of a considerable lack of knowledge.

The only option to avoid that unproductive mood, that would have led me inevitably to a dangerous loop, was "my research folder".

The idea of using "The research file" is always great for a designer. I was taught, finding it useful and essential, to collect along the way of my creative learning, a multitude of inspirational things, such as pictures, scribbles, images, vintage magazines, polaroids, trimmings, fabric scraps, garment references, and set them up nicely into a folder.

It has to contain every type of designer's passions and obsessions, becoming a personal archive, a support, to refer to when there is the need of a concept, topic or just for some fresh ideas.

As my tutor once said, fashion runs fast, so that it is essential to be ready and prepared anytime and produce interesting outcomes. It is almost impossible to always conduct a research from the very beginning without having an idea of the field or concept to investigate, thus the research file will help you selecting one or two themes, that you could easily develop and explore at a later stage.

In that occasion I was intrigued by an Iris Van Erpen creation, with a dramatic look and lots of constructed parts, entirely made of perspex (I supposed).

It was amazing, the only concern was how to reconnect my decision of putting garment references into my mood board, with the world of cinematography. Apparently they did not have anything in common.

I went for a drastic approach, turning the process upside down, and in order to pursue my first "designer scam" I meticulously searched for a film to justify my aesthetic decision of creating a massive jumpsuit with a structural jacket on top.

Once printed out the pictures, and written down some notes and scribbles on them, I started my design development, with hundreds of shape studies, different volumes and proportions, ending up with a constructed silhouette, with tubular legs and a butterfly-shaped jacket on top. The main focus of the second garment, less structured, was its surface resembling a metal armour with two pointed panel placed on the skirt sides.

The drafts were ready, I just needed to connect my initial outcomes to a film, and so I opted for some robots stories, searching for vintage movies which were quite unusual and full of peculiarities. "Tetsuo" was my choice, also called "Body Hammer" produced by Shinya Tsukamoto in 1989, the Japanese cyber punk horror movie was terribly creepy and disgusting in a way, but the garments details and concept behind were pretty responding.

The main issue within my decision of working on that type of clothes, was not only their construction but also the fabric raising itself, so that materials represented a very essential part for the success of the looks.

In that case I was aiming for some transparent fabric, with metallic shades, mouldable properties and stiff texture (almost impossible), and a metal foil, both firm to handle a boned structure, and soft if manipulated and filled with foam.

So, I went to this well-known market, famous for its unconventional supplies, it used to offer a good range of fabrics, colours and textures at reasonable prizes. Materials were probably recycled or kind of industry unused remenants.

"It never disappoints" I thought, indeed I found a very thin fusible laminate fabric, which seemed a proper metal foil, plus a hard cotton (to use as an internal support), but no sign of the transparent one.

My jumpsuit with tubular legs was still a huge question mark, reasonably I decided to avoid loss of time, working on the laminate dress first, that would have taken a considerable amount of hours, while continuing the other fabric sourcing.

To begin with, every garments needs a "flat technical drawing" called "pattern" in real size (body measurements), in order to be cut and then sewn, this process is called "pattern cutting".

You can either use existing blocks (ready-made pattern in size), or create, from the very beginning, your personal one (in standard or in your body's size).

As lots of brands used to do, due to tight deadlines, I followed the same approach of manipulating and developing an actual block, picking the sizes generally used for catwalk models.

At a first glance I was opting for a block 8, suitable for very tall and slim girls, but then I realized I had to fuse and fill the fabric, thus the foam thickness and the stiffness of two materials melted together, would have inevitably affected the garment fit, reducing it approximately by one size, so in my case a 10 could have done better.

I laid down the block on a huge piece of tracing paper, pinned it to the sheet to secure it and avoid mistakes while copying, once sketched the draft I started the real development, changing the position of some darts, adding new ones, emphasizing the bodice volume, with a more curved silhouette, I decided to also create a separate collar filled with foam, cutting the neckline, and enlarging its shape.

Unexpectedly, the "patter cutting affair", was easier than I had imagined, so I had the possibility to proceed straight away with the making of the toile, cutting and sewing all the pieces with the test clothes.

It is advisable to generally cut a calico or muslin first (a cheap fabric which has properties similar to the final one) and check the fitting, shape, seams, edges etc., so that alterations and changes can be made directly on the toile, reported on the pattern, without spoiling precious fabrics and money.

The first garment fitting resulted in a kind of disaster, but luckily that day I had followed the normal procedure for the toile instead of rushing, otherwise I would have used all of my beloved laminates and completely wasted them.

The figure was disproportionated, the length too short and the bodice dropped on one side, I worked for the following four hours, till the studio closure, adjusting and fixing everything, it seemed like a never ending process.

Sunday afternoon

The studios generally had a late opening and closure during weekends, between 1 p.m and 10 p.m, approximately.

The previous day I was close to be kicked out from a security guard, so that I decided to arrive earlier at the doors opening in order to maximise my working day.

The heavenly room full of every designer's needs was nice and quiet, it was a Sunday afternoon and I was completely alone.

The sunlight was passing through the windows, giving the space a warm and cosy feeling.

I used to indulge in my loneliness while working, so weekends were the best moment ever and the most productive for me.

You would reasonably consider unusual not to rest or take a day off work, but in my case, it was slightly different.

"Fashion" meant and still means everything to me, I could not imagine my life without all of these hours and days spent to perfect my crafts, techniques, or to experiment, explore and so on.

It was part of my life, it belonged to me.

I terribly loved my daily tasks, even if I felt lots of pressure (and so I still do), working on them with patience and dedication was the trick.

I placed (actually spread) my bags on a huge desk, took my patterns with all the adjustments and rolled out the fabrics, it was time to cut the final garment.

I started with the foil first, then I moved to the cotton,

adding one centimetre of seam allowance to both, I marked the collar pieces with some notches as a guideline to follow when reassembling all the parts in the sewing process.

At that time I was not totally confident using the industrial machines, they used to struck fear in almost everybody at the very beginning, probably due to their high speed. Some of them, the "Overlocker" were the scariest, not only did they run fast, but also they had a blade to cut the edges of a fabric while the needles were securing it (giving the wrong side of a garment a nice finishing).

I was forced to use the sewing machine at school, I did not yet have a personal one at home, so making the most of what I had, I decided to search for the "right one" which could have helped me overcoming my discomfort.

Among a multitude of sewing machines, there was this old, noisy one, completely forgotten, on the extreme right of the massive room.

Nobody seemed to have ever considered it, apart from me, of course. It was quite slow, with a very rigid foot. "Almost perfect" I thought, enabling me to have a total control of the speed and pressure.

It became "my bestie", we worked for a long time together, always sustaining each other, till the day someone decided to replace it with a more modern one. It was the sad end of our relationship.

Memories apart, I pressed my foot, and the machine started to work, the needle was moving industriously, part by part, dart by dart, the dress was coming to life. I attached the collar to the bodice, leaving a space, kind of hole, to insert my foam and then I did the edges binding.

I was delighted to see my final garment taking shape, I was

finally on my way to complete it, ready to focus on the craved second look.

Meanwhile, the sun was going down, it was almost 9 p.m., and the sky was turning into a deep and intense shade of red.

I powered down the sewing machine and took a stand to check the fitting of the dress.

It was almost done, the filling process with the polyurethane foam was the last thing to do (it took me almost 3 hours, such a terrible and annoying part, and I had the opportunity of being late again, embarrassing myself for the second time with the security guard).

10.30 p.m.

I was dragging a multitude of bags on my way home, and I could not stop wondering whether all of my sacrifices would have been worth it to win the competition.

Honestly speaking, when I was dreaming of fashion I had a kind of attraction for its redundant external image, sparkly and superb, made of ideas, gorgeous garments and shows, instead of taking into account also the hypothetical disadvantages, efforts, strict and tight deadlines, sleepless nights, which are, actually, the "core", an essential part of it.

Behind any great collection there is a strong and structured process, thus ideas and concepts need to be properly developed, otherwise they stay as embryos.

It is commonly believed that a designer's job is mainly focused on producing glamorous dresses, attending exclusive parties and making money, but this is not true, at least not entirely.

Everybody seems to ignore what happens in reality, that is why, nowadays we really need more "behind the scenes" in order to mature a better understand of what the working world is about and how it affects our lives and environment (luckily this new trend and approach is growing within society and consumers as well, producing noticeable effects).

On the contrary, a designer is often forced to constantly come up with ideas on demand in a really short time (as in my case that I had only three weeks to research, explore, develop and make the garments), leading to a life devoted to work, and a mind constantly tuned on catching every stimulus, necessary for the creative process.

Some very exciting parties might also happen, for sure, even if in my case I was still waiting for them. But the real core of "this job" is within the ideas development, the representative touch and efforts you put in it, the peculiarities hidden within your personality that make a garment really stand from the crowd.

It is not only about searching for a nice dress to adorn a body, but also about searching for your personal voice, and what you might want and expect to communicate creating that dress. In order to reach this point, it is essential to pass through hours of experimentations, attempts and failures, improving sensibility, awareness and critical sense, to perfect and progress performances and outcomes.

As a designer, having a range of skills (Photoshop, pattern cutting, sewing, embroidery, knitting etc.) and not merely drawing abilities, is always a good idea, a distinctive feature of your ways of working.

It is an added value that will undoubtedly affect your knowledge and understanding in terms of garment construction, techniques to use, volumes, proportions, finishings, fabric to choose, costs, even when you will not be asked to follow the entire productive process but just the design of a collection.

The weekend was overall productive, so that I woke up on Monday with a nice and positive attitude, I felt confident and proactive. I dressed up fast and left home to start my timely fabric sourcing.

"Marella, this is your lucky day, I can feel the vibrant energy" I kept on repeating.

4 hours later

You could have heard me swearing at the "amazing feeling" I had had in the morning.

I had been spending 4 pointless hours, asking for the impossible and scanning every single centimetre of 5 fabric stores, I was literally giving up, when something caught my attention.

Looking at the street corner, almost hidden by other bigger buildings, there was this tiny shop.

No sign outside, just two dirty windows you could barely see through, but I could notice tonnes of fabrics rolled-up and spread everywhere inside.

I had never heard about this shop before, nor noticed it, but at that point there were no options apart from going in and try to find something interesting.

"Let's give it a go, otherwise you'll end up going at the Uni empty-handed".

It seemed a bit useless to give a chance to the cracky shop, but anyway I decided to knock on the door.

Apparently, nobody was in there, nor the lights turned on, pretty spooky, I pressed the door bell, but nothing happened.

I was about to leave, when all in a sudden a hand came out, seemingly from nowhere, pushing me back a little.

"Good morning" he said.

"Sorry for the wait" he was a nice, good-looking guy in his 30s with a calm and reassuring appearance, he inserted the key in the lock and gently invited me in.

At a first glance, I noticed a kind of screeching note between his friendly approach and the post-war appearance of his ruined shop.

He was wearing a bright and modern suit, and well, the store was falling into pieces, quite an oxymoron.

Turning the lights on, a marvellous yet forgotten treasure came to life, the small little space from the outside was a huge warehouse full of every type of designer's needs, it was a hidden gem (but still run down).

We immediately started a conversation, he showed his professionalism form the very beginning, and a genuine interest for my ideas and concept behind the project.

Reassured by his heart-warming enthusiasm, I decided to share my drafts and sketches, secretly relying on his help.

I felt a kind of connection with him, our conversation was already lasting for an hour or more, and ideas in my mind were becoming clearer.

After having discussed and processed all the information related to the project, fabrics properties, expectations etc., we both had a kind of enlightenment:

"The plisse" we both shouted.

"Oh my god" I thought "It was so damn easy, why didn't it come to me?"

"The plisse is going to give you the perfect balance exactly the way you expect, feminine yet soft appearance plus a nice structure to hide wires and bones as an internal support" suggested Francesco, the store owner, and I could not agree more.

So downstairs we went to carry out our mission, looking for a suitable type of plisse.

"A silent understanding" between two artists: Issey Miyake & Irving Penn. In this amazing picture you can have an idea of how a "plisse" fabric can maintain a soft feeling while producing structural effects. This is the result of an artistic collaboration between Irving Penn (one of my favourite photographer), and Issey Miyake, Japanese fashion designer devoted to pleated garments. Miyake began to experiment with new methods of pleating that would allow both flexibility of movement for the wearer as well as ease of care and production. The garments were cut and sewn first, then pleated.

The term plisse indicates a type of textile finishing given to a fabric, that brings a pleated appearance to it.

The fabric is manipulated almost permanently (accordingly to material properties), placed between a two part mould made of card, and put inside a steaming machine for 25 or 30 minutes, then allowed to cool.

It is possible to obtain a plisse effect via chemical treatment as well.

The main issue within this process is represented by the duration and result of the pleats, thus some natural fabrics tend to lose the folds progressively (such as viscose, linen, cotton and sometimes silk); on the contrary polyester maintains perfect results, staying in place.

This was exactly my point, I have never appreciated synthetic fabrics, especially when it comes to pastel shades and transparencies, so that it was almost impossible for me to make a decision. I was surrounded by 100 % pleated polyesters, and I could not have felt worse.

Francesco, was patient and devoted, tirelessly introducing and showing me every type of options he had in store.

Bobbins and rolls were spread everywhere, laying on the floor, on desks, rested on other fabrics....It was an incredible mess, and definitely "late" for me (I had to run to the Uni).

I felt kind of exhausted that afternoon of my endless research, and also Francesco, having put a considerable effort to help me and sell something, seemed a bit pliable, I expressed my gratitude for his calmness after a terribly deep, time-consuming consultation.

I was the worse customer ever.

Shuffling as a limping, beaten person, I decided to leave,

just needed to pack all of my belongings and offer him a support to clean the disaster we made.

We were both climbing the stairs, when my inquisitive eye noticed a glossy material concealed by several fabrics.

I stopped, instinctively, he starred at me, quizzically.

"Francesco, can you please show me that organza, it is organza, am I right?" I said fearless, risking to be kicked out straight away.

I was pointing at it nervously, revealing my excitement and desperation.

"Which one, Marella? I can't see from here"

"That one" I shouted, I was really rude in a way (shame on me!).

Francesco with his distinctive easy-going approach, tried to get over me but I was already jumping into the rolls, grabbing "my sparkly" organza.

"Ahahahah" He started to laugh " You look so funny, by the way, I didn't get your interest in the fabric considering that you were looking for a plisse".

In that very moment, everything came full circle in my head, that transparent shiny fabric would have been perfect for my jumpsuit, it was delicate, soft enough with its metal-laminate appearance, it was almost "perfect", I had absolutely to make it pleat.

The only concern was its composition, it seemed pure silk, but maybe there was a very small percentage of polyester in it, almost unnoticeable.

"Francesco, it might sound crazy of me, but, is there any chance to have this organza pleated somewhere? How do you think it'll react with the heat pressing?"

I saw his face changing from a surrendered expression to a

desperate one.

"Well, it's a never ending surprise for me today, but I probably have something that could do the job".

"Really?" I replied, lightening up.

He went through his pockets and pulled out a business card. "I knew this factory, which used to do plisse, I worked with them long time ago, 4 or 5 years, they are really serious and professional, but I'm not sure they are still running the business. You know, Marella, it's a very small company, and nowadays especially here, students aren't commissioning this type of things anymore. I don't want to make any false promises, so what I will do is to try and get in touch with them, check if they are still on the market and ask for the minimum quantities of fabric required."

"Francesco, that's amazing, I can now say that I'll need approximately 10 metres of it".

"Brilliant, I think it could work for them".

The positive vibes were right that day, I finally had the possibility of pleating that organza with an astonishing result: Francesco gave me a late night call with the good news and from that moment on we became friends, and his shop a "must-visit place" in case of fabric cravings.

1 week to go till the competition.

There was heaviness in my school.

Everybody seemed to be anxious and desperate, you could have smelled a sense of drama in the air.

We were all working night and day, with the aim of becoming the "next designer to look at", there was a really high competition.

Despite my usual neurotic approach, that time I felt quietly confident in my work, even if not sure about winning.

I had been putting all of my efforts, passion, motivation, dedication, with a "scam attempt as an added value" (shame on me, twice!) for the past two weeks, so I could not have anything to blame myself for.

The pattern cutting process for the plisse jumpsuit was quite difficult, in addition the jacket internal structure made of wires was pretty fragile and required me two more days to fix everything in the right place and seal the cables edges.

The only concern remained the wearability of the look.

I had the impression that the constructed jacket was not that solid once put the metal support underneath, as I was imagining. In addition, during the preliminary fittings it took me more than 3 minutes to fix it properly onto the model shoulder, and it still swung a bit.

I was a little stressed out about this issue, a catwalk generally runs fast, dressing and changing looks is something that could take no more than 30 seconds, so I really had to solve this problem as soon as possible.

The competition was a crucial point for me, in terms of training and accomplishments, it offered me the possibility of having a glimpse at the fashion fast paced environment and its high levels of competitiveness.

There was no space for doubts and inaccuracies. I was forced to improve my existing skills and learn how to manage and solve every type of issue.

In very fast contexts, it is essential to act as a "problem solving" person, having a plan B, C and sometimes also D, to think and react simultaneously in order to overcome difficulties

Close-up of the jacket: As you can see in this picture, taken during the preliminary fittings, the jacket is supported by metallic wires, showing a sense of softness and delicate yet feminine appearance. The transparency of the organza also played a crucial role in order to obtain the desired effect. Balanced, proportioned and positioned in a static pose, but the sleeves point were likely to shift according to the model movements.

and mitigating damages, that normally happen in those occasions.

In the previous three weeks, I had struggled a lot with several complexities, from the garments creation to the catwalk, luckily showing professionalism and boldness, as I was taught by my tutors.

During the fashion show two models decided not to come, and one of them was my choice for the big jumpsuit look.

She was 185 cm tall, enough to wear the look without high heels, as my plan was not to use any. The garment legs were approximately 140 cm long, I had to necessarily cut it in the absence of a girl that tall.

Luckily, as I told you before, I was trained to face every kind of situation, carrying with me "my magic bag", that every designer should have. Inside it, there used to be tonnes of things (a proper travelling treasure), such as: two pairs of high heels (black and neutral), masking tape, stapler, threads, pins, clips, needles, scissors, bondaweb, tights in every colour, nude underwear, glue, socks, paper clips, iron and so on...

It was massive, almost bigger than me, and despite its considerable weight, it allowed me to easily adjust the jumpsuit legs edges with the transparent masking tape, without cutting them off.

Not only did the model change, but also a part of my jacket structure broke 2 minutes before my turn, while preparing my girl for the catwalk, so that I had to replace the left part of the structure with a new piece of wire.

Apart from my "notorious bad luck", my final performance perfectly matched my expectations and dreams.

Experiencing my first ever show, seeing my garments on the

catwalk was one of the most powerful, emotional, beautiful moments of my life.

"Oh my God, it was gorge!"

I was not expecting thunderous applauses, it was a kind of moment of truth, and then...

I could not believe I made it...

I had won the first prize!

The stage was far enough to hide my tears, incredibly happy and grateful, they wanted me to do the final catwalk alongside with my looks, I walked twice, seeing among a multitude of faces cheering me up, my parents. I was not expecting them.

"I proved them my passion was real, I showed them all the love, dedication and hopes I'm putting in this."

I thought, dwelling on their touched expressions.

My mother was almost crying and so was my father, I felt like it was their first sign ever of credit and approval.

I really needed that pivotal point to turn all my desires into something visible, recognisable and noteworthy.

Honestly speaking, I have never felt completely confident about fashion as a life choice, yet I have always let my interests and aims come first, guiding me, without even bothering about having enough potential or talent.

"A talented person, me? Ahahhaha please don't make me laugh", this was my usual answer.

The fact is that, I have always focused more on the journey, rather than where it would have led me, my only certainty was my own devotion.

Commitment does always pay back, it is just a matter of time. I am a strong supporter of this thesis.

It is just "you" to decide how far you want to go, pushing your boundaries, and what really deserves to be pursued.

"Either you take risks or you lose the chance" States a plaque over my study door.

I purchased it for 2 Euros in a kind of bazar, but its value is hidden within the meaning itself, I found it on the worst day of my student life (after a failing project), it caught my eyes probably because I was in desperate need for some "self-confidence injection", and it immediately became my inner compass to look at when I felt lost.

It turned my excitement on, my enthusiasm, my willingness to try harder, to be brave without letting fears and delusions limit my potential.

It has been one of the best "motivator" during my journey, and still it stays hung on every new home I move to, always following me, silently.

After all, I have never had any guarantees in my existence, and neither do you, everything is a kind of "blank canvas", we can either try to paint and adorn it with amazing "drawings" even with some dots, marks and mistakes, or we can ask someone else to fill it for us, making it full of our regrets, fears, and concerns.

Every choice is "our choice", every passion is "our passion", and every work is "our decision" that should make us happy, there is no right or wrong in it.

Choices, they all have the same dignity and fears are part of the game, but do not let them stop us, we should "open that door and go out from our comfort zone", the world is magic out there.

Sure magic was for me that night, with my parents by my side and a nice group of friends, I celebrated all night long in a glamorous party hosted by my University (it finally happened to me, too!)

Our works were all displayed in a massive room on the ground floor, every designer had their own private space, bound between two lateral panels full of every type of clothes, samples and research folders, in the middle of the room a huge, rectangular table towered, set with a delicious buffet.

DJs were playing from the courtyard, creating a really warm and immersive atmosphere.

I was dwelling in an inspiring and engaging conversation with some of my colleagues, between some foods and dance, when the University Dean approached me, to talk about the prize and personally congratulate.

He offered me a monetary prize of the amount of 2,000 Euros, plus the possibility of being featured on a Fashion magazine.

It was a dream coming true, and I can now say I ended my second year in style.

That summer I rested a lot, gathering all the necessary energies to start my third and final year at University.

September 2012, final year.

Since the very beginning, I immediately had the impression that the teaching approach had dramatically changed.

As student of the final year, we were already supposed to be capable of working independently on different tasks with individual processes, so that tutorials were reduced significantly, and tutors shifted to a less spoon-feeding method.

The main focus was preparing us for the demanding and

asked to consider the hypothesis of doing an internship before the end of the academic year to collect more college credits and move into the fashion world in a smoother way. In order to do that we had to think and choose among a number of designers and brands to find out the ones we wished to work for and most liked, or who were most aligned to our ideals, view and design approach. Then proper one-to-one tutorials finally started, giving us the possibility to begin with the "portfolios making of", selecting the best projects we had thus far and producing a number of ideas meeting the image and style of brands we had decided to apply for, while maintaining a strong and representative personality as a designer. We were also expected to produce two versions of it, one digital and the other physical, paying attention to make it both interesting and professional.

Following the works editing and selection classes, there were specific lectures dedicated to resume and cover letters, providing all the necessary tips and suggestions on how to produce them with a distinctive and impressive layout and content.

Everything appeared completely new to me.

I have always believed designers, as all the other workers, should have followed standard and preconceived formats for both their CVs and motivation letters, I have never thought it would have been essential to communicate a unique and personal vision even in written documents.

On the contrary, as a creative it is crucial to show, from the very beginning, who you are and what your "art/fashion" is about.

According to this, the resume has to represent your identity through the layout (colours, formats, etc.), consistently and coherently, in order to catch the attention of the recruiter; in addition, the cover/motivation letter should include your "manifesto" (beliefs, aims, ideals, area of research and creative approach), while showing your interest, commitment and understanding of the Company you are applying for, and capabilities, techniques and knowledge you can bring in the existing business.

Once finished this endless process, lasted for almost 2 months, I finally started "my application phase", sending more than a hundred emails, but for the majority of them, I did not even receive a reply.

Despite my "stalking approach", no company seemed to be interested in my profile, it was pretty annoying and a bit frustrating, but I undauntedly continued for another month, till the first university break.

My last attempt dated 3 days before the Christmas holidays, expecting another dead end, and there it was. Two weeks later, nothing happened, considering that fashion along with Companies were reasonably in pause, due to Christmas time, ergo it was easier for me to cope with that "disappointing situation" of not being considered at all, but I still kept on asking myself whether my portfolio and resume were strong, professional and effective enough.

Luckily, as spending some time with my family and friends had been really rare thus far, I naturally switched my focus to them, enjoying dinners and parties all together.

As a tradition, I used to host a dinner at my place a couple of days before the New Year's eve, with more than 20 friends coming from every part of Europe, it was a special occasion for us to meet and have a relaxed chat, away from our "neurotic" routine and lives. I could not wait to see them all, I was fairly excited and extremely busy in decorating my home and preparing all of the delicious recipes I was planning to cook.

Generally my mother and I were working hard two days before the "event", tidying, choosing the dinnerware, tableware and so on, and my father on the contrary, was desperate for this daily droll, trying to rest somewhere in the house without being defrauded.

It was pretty difficult to reach me during that "pageant", so I used to find hundreds of calls and emails at the end of the day. I was religiously double-checking my phone in the hope of finding any signs or reply from Brands, but nothing, just some updates from my university and some calls from an unknown number.

The following day, I woke up early ready for the "big dinner event", and while choosing the perfect look to wear, I noticed that the unknown number appeared again on my phone display, there were 4 missed calls, plus 3 left messages on my voicemail. The nuisance from the previous night was turning into a proper stalker. It was annoying me more than a little, it felt to me quite intrusive and pushy, especially in that occasion in which I was completely absorbed in my own things.

Determined to manage this situation with the strange annoyer, I called back, ready to fight...but "luckily" no one answered, so the only thing left to me was to listen to my voicemail, while waiting for further signals.

"Good evening, Marella" said a nice and polite voice, quite surprising for such a gross, pushy nuisance, I thought.

"We have received your application, and after an accurate

portfolio review, we finally agreed to have you on board. The fashion week is coming, so we would be delighted with a potential quick start. The company will open on the January 2nd, hope it is not representing a big deal for you and..."

He was still talking, but I could not hear more, I was literally petrified, frozen and shaken and whatever, with my mouth wide open and the phone close to my ear like "The perfect portrait of an idiot".

This is, by the way, another example of my "notorious bad luck".

I have been sending tonnes of emails for the past 3 months, and exactly when I was trying to make other plans, life plans in particular, they decided to consider me, asking for an immediate start!

"Cool".

I felt screwed up as it often happens to me when it comes to fashion.

I needed to sort out that issue as soon as I could, my friends were coming, the table was empty and so were going to be my guests' bellies, had I not started to cook immediately.

So the first "reasonable" thing that occurred to me, instead of making a plan and pack my belongings, was to go in the living room, in my pyjama, shouting: "Mother, I'm leaving" giving to my nervous excitement the possibility to finally come out.

My mum, intent on tiding the sofas, turned her concerned face and quizzically said: "Darling, are you taking drugs? You look terribly weird this morning, and…"

"No, no, mum listen, I got a call, I need to leave".

"Ok" she interrupted me "You are definitely taking drugs!"

"Listen, I have been offered a place as an intern, in a fashion company, but they want me now, I mean, in a couple of days".

"God, are you serious? It's marvellous, Marella!! Then go, go, your luggage are waiting for you, prepare your belongings and fancy looks, I will organise everything for tonight, don't worry".

Seeing the enthusiasm in her eyes, was always a kind of surprise for me, I could not get used to it. She was one of the most "headstrong and conservative" in the family, yet she had become one of my biggest supporters.

Looking at my overwhelmed face in the mirror, I thought that something had happened in the end, I felt completely out of my mind, conscious that perseverance does always pay back.

I had 2 hours to prepare my "departure" before the arrival of my besties, I tried to be as fast as I could dressing up, and selecting some from a multitude of garments to bring with me. It took me almost one and half hours, the amount of luggage was growing indecently, thus instead of a place in the airplane, I should have booked the entire cabin.

Clothing dramas apart, I searched for a flight, and sent an email to my university with the aim of justifying my partial period out, and of course, have their "blessing".

CHAPTER THREE

Scary things: "Going out of the comfort zone"

The purpose behind every Fashion & Arts University is to prepare the future designer generations for the working life, giving students a strong knowledge and understanding of the competitive environment, while helping them building a consistent creative identity.

Despite Its crucial role, University cannot provide a real mock experience, just a coherent background, and for this reason, the upcoming generations often ignore how different processes and rules could be in a company, facing a multitude of difficulties along the way.

When I moved my first steps as an intern, I had to learn once again everything concerning fashion, even though I definitely found essential the skills and techniques previously developed during my studies.

What we really overlook as students is the presence of a different structure within every company, made of a perfect balance between a variety of elements, such as: people, costs, production, timing, hierarchy and creativity, of course. All of these parts are simultaneously interacting, influencing a worker performance, so that it is essential to manage all of them in order to maintain great results.

In particular, fashion is not only about innovative outcomes, but also about networking, sharing, collaborating and respecting authorities and deadlines.

Money and cost, also play a substantial role, affecting brands decisions, and mistakes have a price too, in spite of their undeniable importance in terms of learning. Young professionals are supposed to stay productive and create appealing items, if something goes really wrong within a collection, their whole career in the company might be at stake.

I started at the bottom, manifesting a vivid interest, willingness and enthusiasm.

In the very beginning, it is quite unrealistic to expect of being directly involved in crucial and exciting tasks, it might definitely happen but it does not represent the rule, on the contrary you will have the chance of doing a proper "training period", learning the company know-how, habits, rules, techniques and every type of thing that makes it distinctive and unique.

Commitment and professionalism are both required and indispensable of course, in order to establish a trust relationship with your leader and colleagues.

In my case, the initial phase was slightly boring, as all of you can imagine, I was spending my days designing garments from a template, making photocopies, and adding and perfectly allocating the brand code on a specific sheet part.

It was terribly soporific, but fortunately I was working in a huge open space filled with a plethora of books and boxes with every type of trimmings, accessories, vintage magazines etc., so that once completed my daily activities, I had the possibility of studying from them, losing myself in that enormous knowledge, learning and experimenting.

My investigative attitude immediately caught the attention of my colleagues, who showed their delighted approval poking around, and valuing my drafts and scribbles.

Months were passing in a lovely atmosphere, full of kindness, team spirit and respect, that I had almost forgotten about the apocalyptic scenario people used to describe, till the day I was finally offered a regular working contract.

A nice and obliging intern did not really represent a threat, on the contrary becoming a peer "unleashed the wrath" of my colleagues. Some who had previosuly seemed to appreciate my engagement and dedication started to penalise me, hiding and spoiling my designs, shouting at me for no particular reasons, with the aim of relegating me.

It was the first time I faced how "the negative competition" could perform in the working world.

Instead of being flattered by the outcomes and good performances reached by "the lovely girl" they trained themselves, they preferred to show an envious anti-team work approach. It seemed unreasonable and quite useless of them to discredit me, spurred by the idea that "the new girl would have damaged them all".

I learnt the hard way that "intelligence" is necessary for driving individuals to learn from the others rather than being jealous and disruptive, and that meritocracy is really rare, quite an exclusive prerogative of sharp minds.

The business owner decided to hire a "creative director", with the aim of promoting and boost the brand image, determining a sort of shift in attention from "me" to another "dangerous new-entry", which in that case would have been our "boss".

Rumours, discontent and complaints immediately started, as expected, luckily without really affecting or even bothering him, he was totally concentrated on his challenging tasks, trying to bring more coherence into the different brand collections, penetrate other market segments and produce more appealing yet contemporary garments.

He appeared to me as quite inspiring and supportive, and gladly I became his pupil, learning a multitude of things and dramatically improving my capabilities.

The internal processes and structure were reformed, he set up a fresh and more functional method consisting of two different stages, the first one concerning the team work and a collaborative approach, while the second more focused on individual tasks, developing ideas and drafts independently.

We were supposed to start with a brainstorming, passing through a concept briefing, giving our contribute, opinion and suggestions, in order to finalize the guidelines to follow, after these, we had to start the fabric sourcing, meeting suppliers, making suitable choices and selecting samples, then the creative director would have assigned for each of us a different part of the collection and tasks to work on and further develop before the second briefing.

He included me, since the very beginning, treating me like an established member of the team.

Preparation of the Spring/Summer 2013 collection

The first briefing I joined was mainly focused on trend research.

A cool hunter entered the meeting room with massive books, providing every type of suggestions for the upcoming season.

We scanned religiously each volume, there were notes, socio-anthropological data and tonnes of precious pictures collected during the past fashion weeks and catwalks. There was also a section entirely dedicated to street styles from all over the world, so that a considerable part of the influences and themes were strongly connected and related to people's creative way of wearing garments.

Our Director was kind of obsessed with the importance of streetwear, he was firmly convinced that being aware and conscious of the contemporary era, represented an essential part of the creative process, thus as designers we should have taken into account not only the brand image/heritage, market and related commercial needs, but also social trends, such as: people's tastes, attitude, garment approach and so on, before discussing any optional solution and concept to pursue.

At the end of the meeting, with three themes selected, we had to propose ideas, and support them through visual materials.

Providing a consistent range of images, pictures and references was essential for the creation of a board, also known as "Mood-board", a huge panel containing any type of visual stimulus, such as fabric samples, trimmings, pictures, drafts and so on.

Once prepared it, we would have started the proper and preliminary design development.

In my opinion, the striking difference between working for a fashion brand and studying independently, is not only the time dedicated to every phase, but also the depth of the processes.

As a student I was trained to analyse concepts, deeply explore ideas, and justify them, providing exhaustive reasons (drawings, primary research, pictures) for the decision, style and outcome produced. Therefore, in order to show a great level of coherence within my work, I used to devote my entire days to research, collages, scribbles, objects collection, experimentations, drapings and so on, resulting in an extensive weeks-long process, aimed at investigating a theme from several angles.

On the other hand, the company attitude, was far more different, focused on commercial needs and prone to an aesthetic rather than conceptual approach, it consisted of delimited areas of work: briefing-visual materials-discussion-design-briefing-design (again, when necessary)-samples production-fitting and catwalk.

Honestly the outcomes were nice, but without really showing or meaning anything new. Unsurprisingly banal, in my humble opinion.

Despite the professionalism and experience applied to these procedures, I felt as if a piece was missing.

Not to be pretentious but "sticking nice pictures of contemporary garments, fabrics scraps and colour palette on a huge mood-board" gave me the impression of a rather reductive and basic way of conducting a proper concept investigation, which had fatally led to superficial input and then collection, made of existing garments quotes and already-seen silhouettes.

Ideas need to be supported by the right stimuli, links and inspirational materials, otherwise they will merely end up in a copying process.

Without a consistent research behind, it would have been

very hard not to be influenced by the "mono-thematic images" provided, and that was my case.

At that time, my understanding in terms of design and concept development was not that sophisticated, but the difficulties I faced made me aware of those shortcomings.

After the briefing, my mind was so crowded and full of a multitude of diverse visual inputs.

Although the pictures seemed, at a first glance, apparently linked and connected together, there was not a mood, a purpose to follow, explore and extend so that sticking to the references and details was the only feasible option.

I tried my best to fulfil the director's expectations and suggestions, gradually discovering a hidden need of having a story behind, something that could have guided me through the creative process, actually my outcomes thus far were predictable and boring, almost a disaster (to me).

I felt terribly frustrated, confused, I was completely ignoring the direction to pursue, all of my attempts proved useless.

Unhappy and lost, at some point, I got stuck.

I was sitting on my desk, with a pile of pictures, tonnes of work to do, lots of pressure, but nothing happened.

My head was empty and so were my sheet and feelings, I just got bogged down in that mood.

I was experiencing something called state of "self-sustaining confusion", in which I was no longer aware of what "creative and mechanical thoughts" were, lacking in a clear perception of my reaction and approach.

Being uninspired and feeling blocked is actually the worst, most common thing, that can occur to creatives, designers or to individuals in general.

Sometimes a lack of inspiration could happen without a specific reason, which is definitely normal. In some "bad days" for example, our mind can be unfocused and our attention and feelings belong elsewhere, so it is crucial to give ourselves a break, indulging into natural responses, instead of torturing and forcing responses, without really obtaining any interesting outcomes.

However, in that occasion, my inner inventive verve got lost in fears, desires, aims, insecurities, pleasures and pains, also known as "mechanical thoughts".

These preconceptions and emotions are generally absorbed at an early stage of our existence, conditioning our reactions and behaviour, and twisting the fresh clarity of our mind in a "mechanical way", so that the capacity for originality and creation are deadened and gradually go to sleep, determining a creative block, such as in my case.[4]

That structured yet constrained approach, commonly adopted at the company, led me to an unproductive mood, limiting my mind to a strict pattern, and putting to sleep instead of awakening my inner creativity.

The ideas flow was interrupted by the lack of recognisable stimulus and, most importantly, by the absence of freedom in terms of exploration.

After all, our minds are keen to react creatively to stimulations without conditioning, so the trick is to provide the right ones which are usually different for each of us.

The most helpful thing that occurred to me in that uninspired mood was, first of all, to stop caring, giving space to ineffective

---

[4]   David Bohm, "On Creativity", Page 22-25.

and miserable thoughts. Then, I went back to the source of inspiration and I further developed the images and visual materials on hand, feeling free to find new connections and relations between them.

Dealing with pressure and deadlines might be very difficult sometimes, but sticking to old, impersonal and preconceived patterns or processes with the aim of being faster and more productive, could be fatal for creativity, so that it operates without external and internal constraints. That is why it was essential for me to provide myself with the proper time to go throughout that process.

The more we let others (people, objects, thoughts, processes, insecurities, rules, etc.) intrude our minds, the more we feel blocked.

It was quite a dramatic scenario for me, as it caught me for the first time while I was working. Honestly, I did not have any clear idea on how to proceed, so I took a big breath, cleared my mind and started all over again.

The result of my research was a brand new nourished folder, made up of every kind of shape declinations, taken from the world of architecture, jewellery, art, and every other field which could have elicited emotions in me.

It came handy for my design process, giving me the possibility of avoiding a stated copy of the references provided, and creating something new, mixing and matching fresh ideas.

Unexpectedly, the ideas flow went way beyond the task assigned, thus once finished the sixty garment drawings, I had the insane idea of creating also the accessories for the upcoming show.

All the shapes, volumes and visual inputs accumulated, made me think about a strong, gold and bold collection made of cuffs (rigid bracelets), collars and chockers (stiff rounded necklaces), with references to animals (which were part of the chosen trend).

I did a variety of drafts, coloured and explained them, with proper technical drawings, I clipped all the sheets nicely into small packets and, once finished, I decided to dare, taking the risk, but giving myself a chance. I asked the director to see and discuss my work.

I waited for 2 days before seeing him, until he finally invited me to enter in his room for me to show my coveted work.

"Marella" he said "I really appreciate the efforts you put into this and the audacity of going beyond the assignment given. I think we should definitely consider your proposals, but you need to perfect them, thus it is essential to have a significant number of drawings and drafts to choose from, to eventually select the best for the show".

I could not believe his words: not only did he find interesting my outcomes and approach, but also he suggested further developing my concepts and ideas. I felt proud and delighted at the same time, and almost incredulous. On the one hand I showed reliability and professionalism by completing all of the 60 garment designs previously assigned (during the briefing); on the other hand, I also took my personal investigation forward with fresh new proposals, proving my ability of working independently, thus enhancing a relationship of trust.

Sticking to my personal method, I allowed myself the possibility of exploring and redefining my design development, and this immediately produced noticeable results.

I was aware that passing the line, going beyond the rules and structure, might have costed me a lot, but in the very end, how could have I acted normally, if I was supposed to be a "creative" person, working in a creative environment, and how to have outstanding and impressive outcomes if you are responding to preconceived stimulus, provided by someone else?

Being "creative" also means taking control of your own learning process, questioning, pushing the boundaries, diving inside the things, not merely looking and reproducing their surfaces, and sometimes either going the extra mile, or failing. Inspiration is our inner reaction, something that belongs to us, we should not let anyone manipulate it.

From that day on, the director changed my role, entrusting independent tasks to me, so that I became responsible for the accessories collection, concerning not only jewellery but also shoes, belts and so on, receiving more freedom in terms of research, process and materials choices, as long as my outcomes were aligned to his directions and to seasonal trends.

It appeared necessary to me to make new plans and rebuild my normal work routine, as I was completely alone in managing the progression of my daily tasks, yet totally free to tap into a variety of sources.

Every morning, before going to work, I used to have a look at Instagram pages, to keep regularly up to date with daily proposals and news, and fashion and trend magazines, to write some notes down and direct a preliminary phase of research.

Then, once collected all the necessary materials, I used

to print out the images and organise the folder, connecting themes and visual input, adding scribbles, notes and references, ready to start my design development.

I had never studied accessories design before, which is sensibly different compared to clothes, and an extremely broad field, especially in terms of techniques applied, materials properties and constructions, so I had to expand my understanding and education, guiding my own training and learning from every little thing at my own disposal.

As I told you before, the studio was an inexhaustible source of knowledge, a massive library filled with several topics, subjects and inspiring documents, hence it was easy for me to find very specific volumes on jewellery, shoes constructions, ancient and historical crafts, materials and "making of". Taking advantage of them, led me to a more sophisticated approach regarding shapes and designs, and helped me in producing realistic and comprehensive pieces with technical details, sensible finesse and exhaustive construction-oriented documents (which were generally tasks assigned to technicians dedicated to the production of samples).

At some point, I even felt confident and skilled enough to directly handle a conversation with the lab manager, verbally discussing the best options concerning metal properties and alloys, leather finishings, costs and so on.

My period at the company was undeniably fundamental for establishing an initial working background, and for opening up my mind to a multitude of areas that were still unfamiliar.

From a broader view point, the experience gained, drove me to a more conscious approach regarding the fashion world in general, brands internal dynamics and production processes.

I experienced all the necessary phases and resources involved for a collection, understanding the importance of hierarchies, tasks division, and team support and collaboration.

Before holding in my hand that new and surprising reality, I was firmly convinced of the absolute and prominent importance of the role of a designer in a company, in the absence of which it would have been almost impossible to set up a business.

You know how many "ego-trips" young students could sometimes have, especially in creative fields. I and my colleagues were strictly obsessed with "our key role" as fashion designers,

Spring/Summer shoes collection drafts: Study of shapes and proportions for the S/S sandal collection, patent leather twisted and sewn according to triangular patterns.

kind of godlike figures, deciding the fate of a company, which is in a way partially true, but definitely mythological.

The reason of these unrealistic thoughts needs to be probably sought in a consistent and visible lack of knowledge and experience. Behind the "sparkly fashion world, and mystic power of designers", there is a very complex and sophisticated

Fall/Winter 2013-14: The collection was mainly addressed to strong and powerful women, where black leather, fetish references and samurai silhouettes, were starring.

Corsets with laser-cut stripes made of soft calf-leather were dominating the looks, adding a cheap yet glamorous appearance.

Shoes, strictly pointed and very high (up to 10 cm) represented a perfect balance between fatal femininity, aggressiveness yet softness, thanks to delicate materials and shapes.

corporate structure, in which creative processes account for a very small portion, considering that nothing is left to chance, ideas in particular.

It resembles an "assembly line", where people are not only asked to work on daily tasks, but also to contribute with contemporary and outstanding proposals, taking into account the eclectic, mutable and fast paced environment. Company are subjected to markets rules, and so are designers and all the other employees. So that exploring freely whichever topic, or generating ideas out of touch and beyond comprehension, in contrast with the brand image and heritage, is quite utopian.

In the end, a regular worker even if "operating in the art fields", has to promote and enhance the company image with their professionalism, not pursuing their inner self and individuality, exploring specific themes or conducting independently personal investigations without adding any value to the business.

The ability of a designer consists in diversifying the outcomes according to different collaborations, maintaining a great level of versatility during their career, creating a perfect balance between the company's expectations and their personal touch, taste and creative vision, as a signature of their work.

However, what might also happen to some young designers, at the beginning of their journey, is to either feel trapped, or to unconsciously blend with the company vision, as a result of a still undefined and incomplete creative personality, that needs to be further perfected and explored.

Although I was partially new to this phenomenon, with the passing of the years I realised that every single part of my raw personality was gradually melting away, and even if my role involved independent management of sources, processes and ideas selection, my mind was starting to feel caged by this sparkly yet strict reality.

So it was almost spontaneous for me to start wondering if, working in fashion, would have really been as arty and inspiring as I used to imagine, or if using "creativity" as a proper "work" would have not led to its inner dead.

The fact is that, despite its relation to the world of art, fashion is a social product, regulated by rigid markets and money rules; even if it acts in modernity as a vehicle of political, anthropological, or other inspiring topics, it still remains subject to commercial needs, and preconceived logics.

By definition, creativity and restrictions are ontologically opposed, considering that one should exclude the other, but there is still a possibility to let them coexist together within the same job and operate in different areas of the process, while maintaining a kind of connection in which they gently influence each other.

Freelancer jobs, seasonal fashion/artistic collaborations, and artist collectives, represent for instance ideal situations, in which the designer/artist could perform as an independent figure, accepting some guidelines without compromising their creative input responses, and pursuing at the same time their individual approach without sticking to pre-imposed procedures, nor being distracted by external "dangerous" constraints.

On the contrary, when it comes to a company, being it yours or someone else's, you as an artist will always be forced in a way to meet the business needs, and perfect the related skills, techniques and abilities, sadly limiting your private space for ideas and individual experimentations.

Assuming that a childlike quality of fresh, wholehearted interest is not entirely dead in any of us, we should all be able to have a creative character and approach in our human responses.

Creativity after all, is not about natural born talent, something elitist and limited, it belongs to us all, it is the peculiar way individuals operate. It is the "most personal thing" we have, that acts with similar logics in every individuals, hence producing really diverse results.

Creativity is not merely genius at work: surprisingly, it is about long hours of self-questioning, experimentations, attempts, failures, explorations, rules deconstruction and reconstruction, driven by curiosity and constant need of breaking the schemes and going beyond.

Creatives are nothing less than intelligent people who have recognised the importance of clearing their mind from restrictive dynamics and thoughts, allowing their fresh ideas to flow and guide their responses.

Nurturing and understanding oneself is crucial, to then build a very personal and individual way of processing ideas and data. There is whole world behind every "piece of art" made of a multitude of stimulus, inspirations, studies, investigations, according to our human diversity.

This could be an entire focus on geometry, anatomy, flowers, people and so on, depending on personal tastes, heritage and uniqueness, which is why it is important not to trap different minds into a general "structure and process to follow", so as to avoid flattening all the outcomes, losing their invaluable assortment.

Depriving an artist of their own method would definitely damage their inventive resources.

Can you imagine how frustrating and dramatic could be if, after a lifetime dedicated to explore your inner personality, balancing the creative verve, and discovering who you are as an artist and whom as a person, someone came and force you into being and acting in a different and impersonal manner?

Meanwhile I was dedicating all of my efforts to the brand, leaving the necessity of structuring myself behind.

My outer shell was not that strong nor yet formed at that time, important pieces were missing, such as a deep understanding of my interests and obsessions, my ego, and defined methods of conducting my creative research. I was still stumbling around, letting the feelings guide me.

Honestly speaking, I was at the beginning of my journey, so that terrible doubts were taking roots into my mind.

Despite being genuinely grateful for the working opportunity given, I was also terribly aware that pursuing my own development, continuing my studies, would have led me to a much more satisfying condition. I was in desperate need for discovering my inner self as a designer, I felt as I could have no longer waited.

2 months later

In a warm and quite afternoon, I was chilling at my usual working station, with a historical book in my hands, observing the rare garment pictures, when Antonio, one of my colleagues, suddenly entered the room.

It was probably a couple of weeks after the show, the mood

was pretty relaxed, everybody finally rested a bit, trying to get rid of the stressful and neurotic pre-catwalk attitude.

I was surprised to see Antonio shaken in such a lovely atmosphere, he walked to my desk and rudely closed my book.

"Marella, hurry up, the brand owner wants to speak to you! Go to the third floor, he is probably already there, waiting for you in room C15".

"Oh… ok, then". I said, standing up and leaving the room as soon as I could.

I had never visited the third floor, it was kind of a forbidden area, and I could not hide a sense of electric excitement.

The door was slightly ajar, giving me the possibility of peeking a bit before knocking. A massive and elegant desk was standing right in front of me, the owner sitting on an opulent design chair on the right, with a pile of sheets close to his arm.

Then came the anxiety... I was wondering about the content of those documents nicely piled on the desk.

"Oh god, maybe I made some mistakes during the show, or probably some accessories didn't have a good market feedback…"

I was already starting to punishing and tormenting myself with disruptive thoughts, I also considered the hypothesis of running away, but something stopped me.

Can you guess what?

My curiosity, of course.

I wanted to know so badly what those hidden sheets were all about.

I knocked on the door, and a polite voice suggested me to come forward.

I could not see any emotions, expressions, or positive vibes on the owner's face, and spontaneously I decided to prepare myself for the worse.

After a couple of minutes, a discussion started about my performance, with a proper evaluation of goals achieved, improvements. Then he moved to more critical aspects, underlining my weaknesses.

Once finished his analysis, he made a pause, remaining silent for an uncomfortably long amount of time, and a bad feeling sneaked up on me.

"He has been trying to prepare me for the end of the contract, otherwise why should have him discussed my lacks and weaknesses?" I thought.

My worries were drastically interrupted by his gentle and calm voice: "Marella, after having considered and evaluated your outcomes, taking into account also your inexperience and young age..."

He took a pause and grabbed a sheet of paper from the pile, positioning it in front of me with a pen: "we all agreed that it would be convenient for you to interrupt the existing collaboration contract and..."

Instead of listening to his speech, I was canvassing the entire sheet in a desperate need of finding some answers, so I turned the page and the heading made me jump.

It was an "open-ended contract", that's why the owner suggested not renewing the previous one!

tonnes of thoughts invaded my mind, I felt proud of what I had accomplished and flattered by that proposal, already dreaming of me as a very young designer hired, with a secure job as all "normal" professionals.

My parents would have been so delighted of this, I would have proven them and people in general my skills and capabilities, I would have finally deserved consideration and respect like all the others, but...

On a different perspective, actually "my very own perspective", I was too terribly young to stop my curiosity and give up the need of exploring and knowing the world of fashion.

I was not done.

I felt the necessity to continue with my studies, to experience diverse realities, and find people to share ideas with who were similar to me, I was not ready to surrender my aims and hopes, not yet.

Not at that time.

I could have not made a decision based on others' desires, insecurities and fears. It is me walking in my shoes, I am the only one who can either benefit or regret from the decisions made.

So, with a clear idea of what to do, I decided to point straight into the scariest and most unexpected direction ever.

I politely waited for the end of the owner's speech, then, I turned the offer down.

And I left.

CHAPTER FOUR

Learning:
a never ending process

"*We all need to adopt a lifelong approach to learning*"
That was my belief at that time, and in order to progress in that direction, it seemed necessary to go one step further, moving out of my comfort zone.

I was out looking for my inner voice as a designer, and for unleashing the creativity I knew was hiding within me. Years of high school, micro-managed learning and strict productions, had numbed it all, so that, getting it out again, was almost impossible for me.

I had to switch to a very creative system, which would have required a reformation itself.

Because, you know, education, whether it is business or fashion etc., should be about learning and nurturing the whole human, not only the brain, much in the same way kindergarten does.

We really need creative learning, regardless of age and topic, and a new approach to it. Ignoring it, we risk to be left behind, considering that we are all experiencing how drastically the global landscape is changing in our lifetime, especially in fashion. So either we keep up with it, taking part in these changes, or we rest obsolete, but in order to do this it is essential to constantly evolve ourselves, and experiment freely.[5]

Despite the clear need and the conscious urgency of continuing my creative growth, the idea of moving back to study, after years spent working in the fashion industry, made me feel a bit reluctant.

I kept on wondering what might have added another "deep immersion" in an academical environment, how it could have affected and changed my performances, and if another "strict-to-the-rules-approach" would have definitely opened my eyes to unconventional realities and new perspectives. Due to this conflicting feelings, I also contemplated the hypothesis of just perfecting my crafts and manual techniques, attending some workshops or short-term courses, leaving aside, for a second, the importance of developing my raw creative persona in its wholeness, not merely focusing on some specific lacks I had.

To clarify all of my doubts, I started an exhausting and consuming research on line, aiming, this time, for the best options available worldwide, fashion schools with outstanding and unconventional teaching methods internationally renowned

After a preliminary check, three names appeared to be the most influential in the academic panorama, situated in different countries.

The first one, which caught my attention since the very beginning, located in London, UK, had an undisputed strong reputation, due to the incredible list of successful alumni, and its very peculiar methodology. The second one, was a Parisian Academy, while the last an American school of arts in the flourishing New York.

---

5   Patrick Mc Dowell, "1 Granary", Instagram page.

These three appealing Universities were staring at me, equally high-value, modern and prestigious, but something about the London school triggered an unplanned sense of fear and excitement in me.

Its name, heritage and history got me emotional.

While having a look at the course programs, the internal spaces dedicated to workshops and tutorials, the machinery offered, its culture itself, I had the impetus and a fervent desire of applying immediately, taking part and actually being part of that incredible, inspiring reality.

The school was offering a vast range of courses and programs, capable of satisfying every student's needs. There was a classic BA, which lasted 4 years, foundation courses to help channeling young artists into a specific, desired field, tonnes of short and part-time programs, plus two post-graduate options, with different duration.

Considering my already long and strenuous academic history, I instinctively opted for a post-graduate course, pretty confident about my background, overlooking the school strict eligibility criteria.

I was determined.

As soon as I downloaded the application form, I filled it out in a moment, and booked a flight for London to attend the first part of the interview.

June 2015, London

"What I have always appreciated the most about London, is that period of time between May and July, that gives to the city a really warm and poetic appearance".

The air filled with spring fragrances, the pleasant breeze which let you indulge out in a night walk, the intense chattering of people around pubs, this festive, relaxed atmosphere that speaks about a re-born phase, a tranquillity after a "wintry thunderstorm".

It was my second time in London, after a previous terrible visit, which unhappy memory still scared and shook me a bit, and the lovely, welcoming atmosphere immediately embraced me. I was prepared for the worst, imagining myself overwhelmed by anxious and scary thoughts and feelings; on the contrary, far from my expectations, a positive vibe took me over, since the very beginning.

My accommodation was near Saint Pancras station, and I decided to reach the hotel on foot, surrounding myself with this vibrant energy.

The streets were a melting-pot of styles, languages, people, activities and ethnicities, like several micro cosmos coexisting all together and interacting at the same time.

I felt full and inspired, there were so many things to look at, and so many places to discover; but the initial excitement, was brutally wiped out once arrived at the hotel.

I pressed the bell and an incomprehensible voice shouted.

" Hello" I said, trying to introduce myself.

"Hi, wrscvsnfju and sfhekfbfjfkpieh to sfshdbck [...]".

I could not properly understand any of its words, I felt so pissed off...

The alien and demonic sound, was nothing less than the British language, terribly new to me. Despite my friends' recommendations and assurances that hours and hours spent watching english TV shows would have definitely been useful in terms of learning, and that, after this kind of "video marathon", "the language" they said "will come to you, Marella", but when in need, no words came to me, not even a question mark!

The only thing that occurred, after that instant crash to this unknown world, was the desperation and the panic!

" How can I communicate with people? And above all, how can I manage to attend the interview tomorrow, in this condition?" I kept on asking myself, terribly frustrated and disoriented.

Meanwhile, the gentle alien of the hotel decided to reach me, downstairs, and let me in, reasonably noticing that something went wrong during our first attempt of conversation.

Like a "fish out of its bowl", lost and upset, I had the impetus of going back to the airport, take the first flight and leave, putting in jeopardy all of my intentions, aims, beliefs and efforts.

"Everything new sounds weird, scary and uncomfortable".

Believe me or not, facing a new reality while leaving miles away your own roots, heritage, traditions and habits which have been accompanying you for a lifetime, is terribly disruptive (at the beginning).

The fact is that we are so steeped in our culture to sometimes forget to caress the idea that there is a whole world out there, dramatically different yet humanly similar that deserves to be explored, lived and appreciated; and at first glance, I would also dare with the thesis that not only do we undervalue the potential and beneficial aspects of so doing, but also the difficulties, sacrifices and efforts likely involved in it.

The truth is that differences, whether they refer to culture, language or traditions, are a great vehicle to promote self enrichment, but in case of mismatch, can also be barriers. So the process of integration takes a lot, a massive, reasoned effort, a positive attitude that needs to counterbalance feelings of frustration, isolation and loneliness that can sometimes appear. As in my case, I was experiencing a typical crisis, due to the inability of expressing my thoughts, myself.

It is undeniably uncomfortable, the first time, although it represents just another part that constitute our "life precious learning process", that will lead us to a more ductile mentality, eager to appreciate rather than discriminate, to take risks rather than comfortably lounge while feeling done.

Unfortunately that night, there was no space in me for a well-reasoned intellectual approach, just for dramas.

I was not contemplating "the failure" as an option, nor the necessity of being patient and calm, indulging in an unconscious narrow attitude, that made me too proud and secure about my work (apart from the obvious language uncertainties), instead of wisely aware.

A thoughtful perception of the school, of the new reality in its wholeness and the highly competitive environment, was clearly missing. My understanding was partial, and the massive gap between my previous experience and that multicultural world, standing right in front of me, should have awoken me that night, driving me to honestly envisage the occurrence of a failing, and if so, elaborating a B plan.

Day of the interview.

The day of the interview, did not exactly go the way I was expecting, actually, slightly different, indeed it resulted in a complete disaster.

Not only did I forget some relevant pieces of work to show, but also my process and outcomes were judged as inadequate, poor and miserable.

As soon as I entered the building, I was kicked out, straight away.

I could not take the time of poking around, grabbing helpful information, nor having a look of my peer's works, noticing the striking disparity compared to mine.

It was a uprising and instant crash.

BOOOOOM!

I stepped outside the school, empty-handed, finding myself immersed in a huge square, that I had completely ignored in the morning.

I was in the middle of an enchanting space, full of lovely spots, enclosing its perimeter, with modern unusual fountains placed in the centre.

These contemporary cascades, resembling to an art installation, were alternately moving, with the rhythmic sound of the water lapping on the concrete floor.

Stolen by the scene, with a drained mind, I indulged in the quiet and surreal place.

It seemed as if time had stopped, apart from the tireless flow of the fountains, which was the only sign of movement in the almost static landscape.

I took some rest, sitting down on the tepid ground, indulging in that "incessant march", contemplating this new sense of infinity and calmness I was snatched by.

After all, I was no more in a rush, there were no appointments to attend, nor things to do.

I needed to stay with myself, in silence.

For an undefinable amount of time, my head remained empty, thoughts did not occur, and I could enjoy, for the first time, the greatness of the void.

Me, sitting on the ground, as a small little black point in that immense, heavenly scenario. Trees and plants were shining under the lazy sunbeams, students were chilling on benches, and the sound of the fountains was echoing undaunted.

I would have stayed there, forever.

It would have been my place.

But was it still the right place for me, after that unfortunate event?

The unpredicted rejection of my application, produced an inconceivable transformation within myself. It forced me to go out my shell, and open my mind far more, once again.

My constant obsession of creatively rehabilitating my persona in order to satisfy my previous social environment expectations, led me to massively deploy all my efforts in the wrong direction.

Instead of merely focusing on my capabilities, progressions and growth, I felt distracted by a consuming, exhausting fight I had personally endorsed, against myself, that, in the end would have never seen any winning.

I had been restlessly pushing my boundaries, without really knowing and understanding where to, any of my final goals, I had been too busy trying to fill and cover all of my holes, lacks and insecurities, to effectively allow myself the time of taking a break and analysing with a wise, neutral vision my performances, thus far, what I needed to improve, what to search for and what made me passionate about.

I was so much into "proving someone else I was enough", that I had primarily forgotten it with myself.

Despite the fierce love always showed for my dream, and the efforts and reasoned choices made, this painful, counterproductive scheme was still hiding in me, waiting to come over. Needless to say, at the point reached, I was seriously contemplating the idea of giving up, forsaking the craved University.

I could have not accepted this crash with my intimate self, especially considering that I had been growing with a perpetual sense of inadequacy, I did not have the structure to deal with it without triggering, once again, a meaningless loop, made of, insecurities, self offences, etc.

Deeply imbued in myself, suffering past memories and patterns, I realised that, this dangerous attitude in approaching problems, would have condemned me to certainly miss several valuable pieces of my life.

The truth was, I was literally scared.

Silently convincing myself I was not enough, acting coherently, I was too afraid of trying and proving me wrong.

The harsh feedback obtained, woke me up, shook me from my numbness, and probably that painful comfort-zone.

The unhappy episode, marked a transition from a still raw, constrained perception, to one, more mature and aware, of me as a person; but the doubts still remained.

How to get over this unremitting internal process?

How to conduct a neutral self evaluation from a broader external perspective?

How can an individual be that open minded and free from human feelings, social influences and restrictions?

In order to reach this "mindful status of grace", we should firstly embrace our whole being, as it is.

Only accepting our nature, we shall be able to detect our lacks, enhance our potential and improve our skills. It is like a continuous process of learning, re-learning, defining and refining, without ever stopping; but this for sure, represents the trickiest part.

Conflicts and confusion naturally inhabit our minds, so it seems very challenging not to be influenced by them, and guided into preconceived perceptions of ourselves. They generally wheel our emotions and decisions into unsafe patterns and directions, feeding a sense of frustration, fear, indecision and so on.

In my case, I was permeated by the general scepticism about fashion and creative jobs, too obsessed with the impossibility of failing, so when it came to getting prepared for the interview, instead of putting myself out there, checking the requirements, looking at other alumni's portfolios, and pausing on my lacks and necessary adjustments to do, I just felt proudly done. And I failed.

I refused to face the scariest part hidden within my reluctant behaviour, namely "my smallness"compared to all the others that had successfully completed their post graduate course, inevitably losing the opportunity of learning from them, and selling my work in a more effective way on the due date.

I preferred to expose myself to an hypothetical crash, instead of handling the situation in a responsible and conscious manner.

And so my lack of confidence did the work for me, driving me to fail, and taught me a crucial lesson.

In the months following the inglorious performance, I had

been searching a lot from the School exhibitions, catwalks, events and initiatives, progressively discovering an unplanned reality made of noticeable, conceptual pieces.

Garments and arts in general, were substantially different from my expectations, and the creative environments I had been exposed to.

Experimental textures, structures beyond imagination, unusual finishing and above all, variety, were shouting out loud from those pictures. I was astonished, scrolling the internet pages, secretly understanding the reason of my rejection.

" How could have I been so blind, presenting my poor portfolio to them?" I thought, this time showing a new form of honesty, also known as "critical sense".

Once moved the first steps into this beneficial aware part of my persona, I felt the urgency of something to cling on, a written feedback, a contact that could have established, even if partially, a connection with them. I wanted so bad to study there, I did not want for any reason and any catastrophe in the world to put in jeopardy my chances of getting in!

I asked for a remote evaluation and explication of the work presented, and there it was, the longest, largest worst list ever of my ineptitudes.

I supposed, they had tried to "sum up" at their best my creative attitude and designer's skills, or should I say my weaknesses, poorness, lacks, incapacity and so on as a designer!

One thing was clear, I caught in its perfection and wholeness, the idea they had matured of my persona, as a big, consistent piece of crap (very picturesque, considering their inner imaginative verve)!

Honestly speaking, after having read with meticulous attention every single line of the full-bodied evaluation, I instinctively had the impetus of jumping out the window, but my flat was at a ground floor, and I would have ruined all of my father's precious delicate roses!

I decided to go through this process of complete deconstruction with the purpose of further improving my skills, capabilities, and in a way to let new aims and beliefs flourish.

I underlined all the "key words" contained in the document, taking notes of the multitude of lacks, gaps I had shown during the interview, that necessarily needed to be filled. I also paid deep attention to the suggestions offered in terms of concepts explorations, ideas development and garment presentations, with a more critical sense alongside me.

I realized the necessity of searching for a kind of preparatory course, firstly to compensate the insufficient background, and then to allow myself to smoothly try once again, this time from an "internal position", benefiting from the common techniques, creative approaches and methodology used in the School.

Scrolling the University official website pages, I found interesting options, vary and complete, the majority of the courses presented a short duration, and a specific field of studies, such as: Pattern cutting, moulage, experimental draping etc. Despite their undeniable appeal, they did not match my needs, nor expectations. I was looking for such a "total make over", mostly focused on portfolio preparation and design processes.

I was literally losing my faith, when a long-term fashion program caught my attention.

On a broader perspective,with a preliminary look, its main focus appeared to be a kind of re-organisation of the student works already produced, which in my case would have represented just the tip of the iceberg, considering the evident lacks I had. Then, I read carefully about its structure, duration and aims along with some alumni interviews, realizing that the objective of this highly intensive program was, not only to produce a school portfolio necessary to apply for other courses, but also to push students' understanding of fashion, channelling their preconceived ideas of how to design garments. Visual research, experimentations and concept development combined with unique presentation skills represented the core of it.

Students were expected to work hard and find inspiration in new, unexpected places, both real and imaginative, identify their own strengths and weaknesses, whilst learning to overcome personal limitations.

Its presentation left me with a very positive feeling, due to its exhaustiveness and attractiveness.

I decided to give myself a chance.

Before applying, I prepared four small projects, this time with a different overture, having learnt a clear lesson from the previous event, and luckily they were accepted.

The course, would have been my skeleton key to progress and live up to my craved Post-grad.

10 months later

I felt still on the line, whilst embracing the change completely, without regrets.

I was conscious this time.

The portfolio course was due to start in a couple of days, and despite the wise approach adopted over the past few months, I was reasonably nervous yet thrilled.

I was wondering if the competitive level was significant, the understanding of the language manageable, my English fluent enough to present the projects, and the unusual method effective. Honestly speaking, the barriers within communication represented to me one of the scariest part, considering the due limits of a person who is experiencing its first relocation.

On the other hand, I filled my scary self with a sense of satisfaction and gratification for the goal achieved, and the resolution shown.

The opportunity offered was unique, not only to build and unleash my creative verve, but also to establish a proper fracture with the old, constrained mentality I had been exposed to.

My head was full, crowded, weary, and so my arms were.

Gripped by that whirlwind of thoughts, I completely disconnected from the piteous tasks I was doing: carry on three huge luggages all alone, at the airport.

It was late at night, but the airport seemed to be at the peak of its activity.

The astonishing throng was flapping convulsively, there was no space to move.

A bunch of noisy people, deeply intent in talking, cluttered my way, without even noticing me limping and swearing with my heavy bags. One of them, I suppose the brightest one, stepped backwards completely absorbed in his thunderous laugh, and hit the already fragile luggage turret. I saw the bag on top flying away, over my head, over their heads, to then crush on the floor, opening and spreading my belongings, included the underwear, all over the place.

It resembled like a flea market!

"Great start, London, I'm like... I already hate you!" I said, mumbling out loud.

I was furious.

After the initial "Spartan Race" between people and complexities, I finally found my cab, at the airport exit, waiting for me and.. can you guess what?

The driver was holding a massive sign supposed to have my name on it...

"I can't believe thi!! Who is Meralla?? Am I supposed to be her??? Oh god, these British people!!"

The driver showed his calmness and extreme comprehension when I tried to remark that my name was MARELLA, not Meralla or whatever.

Laughing in his sleeves, his lovely amused face turned into a scared expression when it came to arranging my heavy luggages..

"Ahahah, I have the last laugh" I thought!

The ride lasted for an hour, and then I finally reached my new place.

It was so lovely and warm, and the bed, well, it was huge.

Once opened the room door, I could not stop myself from jumping on it.

Enrolment day

The email sent to every student, suggested to arrive 15 minutes before the enrolment time. So I decided to take it easy, being there half an hour before, having the opportunity to chill a bit in the paradisiacal square.

I was excited and electric.

"The day I have been waiting for so long, has finally arrived.. I could have never imagined I would have made it!" I thought.

A weird, unusual feeling took myself over, experiencing for the first time the benefits of making a decision, facing its accomplishment, while being proudly confident and conscious that there are no limits, for those who want to persist and insist.

The reassuring perception accompanied me for the entire "enrolment process". Being suspended in a kind of warm cocoon, I felt as nothing could have really shaken me.

The waiting time was interminable, as the long line, formed at the entrance of the building, was.

The student assortments appeared remarkable! Not only the style and fancy looks, but also their extreme variety in terms of ethnicities, heritage etc., there was this scent of internationality, of attractive cultures, scattered in front of my eyes. My heart was submerged with a joyful emotion, and a bit of undeniable apprehension.

The multicultural environment was new, and quite utopian for me, as opposed to the narrow and flat reality I had been exposed to. In my home town, people were keen to judge others, based on their appearances, aesthetics, as a proper result of a "non exposure to the world facets", so reasonably, once compared myself to this multitude of personalities imbued with stories and experiences, in all sort of exotic combinations, I felt almost dizzy.

After two long hours, the intricate and complex process came to an end, and with my brand new student card, I was given a map to reach the precise location of the course.

It caught me by surprise.

The immense warehouse, I had been craving for 10 long months or more, actually was not supposed to be our venue.

"But it's not fair!" I thought.

However, despite the relocation of some fashion programs, all students would have had access to the main building, benefitting from its facilities, such as the massive library, internal art shops, cafes, machinery rooms and fashion studios.

The headquarter of the portfolio course, was located in a small modern flat, encircled by an imperious compound, almost disappearing in it. It could be barely seen from a block distance.

It was immersed in an intimate spot, in the middle of a crowded London borough. Next to the corner a tree-lined street, opened, with enchanting cafes and bistros, giving the impression of a Provençal small little town.

Cars hardly passed, and people were comfortably enjoying a recovered sense of relax while walking in the centre of the street.

Everything was so cosy and welcoming.

10 a.m.

All student entered the building, reaching their new work-position.

We were supposed to occupy the second floor, in which there were squared and bright spaces, articulated by long desks, photocopiers, computer-stations and projectors.

We were guided into the biggest room, on the right hand side of the floor entrance, whilst six picturesque tutors, standing in the middle of it, welcomed us, briefly introducing themselves.

It was possible to hypothetically assume their personalities just from their aesthetic choices.

The youngest, were more into streetwear, promoting a fresh yet personal interpretation of the contemporary trends; the male, more pompous, seemed to be kept to himself, while the female definitely friendly and sunny, had these amazing green eyes.

The scariest, the course leader, was tall, middle aged, warm dark skin tone, brooding attitude and a funny beanie on a side of his head, completely dressed in a light shade of blue. He wore this jersey squeezed jacket, partially closed, and a very compassionate expression on his face, resembling the "Gioconda".

I was inexplicably impressed by him since the very first day, needless to say he became my favourite one, my reference point, my mentor, the one I would never want to disappoint.

His right-hand man, mainly focused on administrative tasks, was shorter than him, embracing a kind of "Yamamoto style" with vivid and astute eye and an undefined age.

Slightly leaning on a desk, two last women were canvassing us with inquisitive interest.

My attention was caught by a lovely expanse of purple hair. There was this lady, probably the oldest among them, terribly charming, wearing a colourful kimono, richly and finely made, in silk, matched with printed pants, bright and multicoloured as well.

She was radiating this poetic mix between Indian and Japanese culture, the characteristic allure of oriental distant lands...being in complete contrast with the severe and alter figure next to her.

Last, but not the least, was a kind of "victorian dame", completely dressed in black, with a voluminous skirt and ruffles all over. Her pale, pearly skin resembled porcelain, and her long blond straight hair, delicate silk threads. She was quite intimidating.

That day we were given glimpses and insights of the course and teaching methodology, plus a list of materials to carry in the following days.

This world, beyond my imagination, reasonably disoriented me. Teachers, were iconic, weird, diverse and informal, without showing anything in common with the stereotypical "academic allure".

No signs of formal approaches, nor the presence of strict university patterns, just a pure strong focus on the importance of learning, working hard, and maintaining and nurturing students' individual multiplicity.

All of the sights were set on us.

Tutors were tastefully dwelling on our personalities, digging and suctioning every type of information, and sign of distinctiveness.

Their vivid eyes, pointed straight into our direction, breaking the external reefs and muscling in our substance, they were detecting our nature, background as a kind of x-ray procedure.

According to this inquisitive approach, their teaching method would have been as sharp as appropriate for each of our peculiarities, diversities and individualities.

In a number of work environments, as well as in several Academic scenes, the importance of adopting and boosting a consistent stance as an "informal sharp leader", rather than a "canonical boss", is generally not under consideration.

What is largely taken into account, on the contrary, is the prominence of "being in charge", of " calling the shots", overlooking the core and potential hidden within those roles.

Therefore, a noticeable gap exists between "leader" and "boss", both in terms of semantic nuances and working attitude.

Leaders mostly focus on the individuals' development, operating on a sophisticated and psychological sphere within social contexts, so that the discovery and enrichment of human assets becomes crucial, as a key element for the pursuing of "targets".

The negligence of an anthropocentric vision, on the other hand, would prejudice results and performances, whilst showing all the limitation of a standardized, obsolete, unproductive approach. The attainment of objectives should never prevaricate the human side, just like a pushy motivational attitude should never overcome an inspirational one; otherwise several negative aspects might occur, creating a typical scenario that "bosses"experienced at least once in their lifetime.

The act of conducting, needs to move towards a positive and beneficial direction rather than an oppressive one, thus channeling is not merely ordering, by contrast it considers a number of different facets, from individuals responses to object features and traits.

It would be far more effective if a tailored-made method, according to human variety, would be adopted and embraced in its wholeness, in order to promote high levels of productivity, plus a proper enhancement of the precious potential undisclosed in each individuals, preventing the flattening of resources

After all, letting somebody reflect rather than instructing

them, represents an indisputably more complex process, but definitely far more fruitful.

Great leaders have emotional intelligence, sharp minds, empathy, are empowered by influence, capable of "making the most out of what they have"(people included), starting from a careful observation and evaluation of different elements, such as our Tutors did with us.

Based on all this, it appears crucial to develop and maintain a pure, vivid interest and humanity, with the aim of establishing trust relationships, especially when it comes to "training students".

The strictness of patterns and rules, without encouraging a deep understanding behind, and the impossibility of questioning and developing a personal methodology, could compromise the flourishing of ideas, the individual growth and confidence, whilst suppressing unique reactions, producing a kind of "atrophied state of mind" among youngsters.

As to guarantee a consistent and aware progression, an inclusive, engaging attitude is advisable, since all human beings secretly nurture the desire of being involved, considered, appreciated, and young generations in particular, seriously need to be stimulated in a constructive and open-minded way.

The importance of hierarchies and rules cannot be denied, for sure, but they should also be called into question sometimes, with appropriate acts in support, promoting the flourishing of creativity and newness.

"First learn the process, to then challenge, experiment and subvert it"aligned with ideas turnover and progressivism.

Students are the future, our future.

It is essential to help them build and mature a conscious point of view, a proactive attitude and a curious and investigative *eye, so that they could question, evaluate and understand the world out there.*

" I've always believed you have to have the skills before you destroy them. A lot of people think they don't need to know the history, and that create newness. I disagree: we should always be informed and then destroy it." [6]

"It is believed in fact, that those who don't learn from history, are doomed to repeat it, wasting a wealth of inspiration. Careful study of bygone eras, or the current one, can lead designers to consider how they may be able to best define the times they are living in." [7]

After the initial briefing and tools/equipment list, we were given a task, to work on at the beginning of the week.

The main focus was the collection and research of "cool faces", "impressive fashion poses" and "interesting fashion illustrations".

Completely overlooking the inner sophisticated purpose of the assignment itself, I approached this aware, delicate phase of selection in a too superficial way " Such an easy thing to do, definitely weird for the best school in the world" I thought (ignorance is bliss!).

The following day, the young male tutor, Jack, would have checked our work, guiding us towards the first two weeks of creative learning.

Starting of the course

"Good morning folks, have you been searching for the best

---

[6]   Louise Wilson.

[7]   Jay Calderin, "Fashion Design Essentials".

pictures ever? I'm going to start looking at your research piles from this desk, moving on progressively by order"said Jack, pointing straight into the far left of the room.

"Please, lay out your sheets, divide them into 3 groups, so that the evaluation process is going to be faster and easier for everybody. Oh I forgot to say, from now on, tutorials will be public, it means that the entire class will be actively involved; we will discuss all together each of your outcomes, so that the learning process will pass through the analysis and view of the variety of your work. It is essential for you to follow me towards each desks, whilst enriching yourself with new perspectives, different solutions and approaches, developing at the same time a critical sense, which is a key ingredient to progress and guide your own learning. The ultimate goal is, while following the suggestions given, to push your boundaries, discover your raw persona, being open, socially conscious, and critically capable of perfecting your skills and capabilities."

The "evaluation" process started, being overall tough, honest and frustrating.

The majority of us came with an "empty gesture", having completely overlooked the core of the task.

Jack was reasonably disappointed, looking for coolness, inspiration and weird attitude within the images provided, he only found basic and banal choices.

The existing difference between the common sense of "fashionable" and this fresh upcoming new mentality, strongly embraced by my tutors in general, which was celebrating individuals, really struck me.

Jack, was undoubtedly looking for peculiarity within a face, personality, signs of distinctiveness, vibrant attitude, things that a "standardized and stereotyped beauty", such a kind of ridiculous combination of all the elements largely accepted for capturing imagination and seeking consensus, could not have provided for sure.

He was searching into individual uniqueness.

"Plastic perfection" nowadays, is becoming obsolete, meaningless, futile and alienating. In the fast paced era we live in, the attention is moving towards the re-born importance of story-telling, of participating to the social issues and dynamics, of speaking out loud and having a point of view. That is why, human variety, its heritage, different roots, are so important, representing in a way the inspiring mixed culture of our time, that has a new voice; resulting to be far more appealing compared to the anonymous mute, flat, old-fashioned icons who do not add nor tell anything new, apart from their aesthetics.

We are all craving for cool vibes, confidence, substance and action, especially in fashion.

Up until that moment, I had never paused, with a careful inquisitive eye, on the inner sense, the energy concealed within a picture. On the contrary, I had kept myself busy to categorize them into nice and ugly, completely missing the possibility of detecting and noticing striking details, peculiar elements, moods, attitude, etc.

I had been terribly superficial, with a mind completely set on a very old scene.

Here, in London, the fashion panorama was eclectic, vibrant, energetic and, most of all, "young".

A plethora of teenagers were committing to contemporary

Ibrahim Kamara & Kristin-Lee Moolman (The Museum of Modern Art, New York).

Stylist Ibrahim "Ib" Kamara purposefully explores and subverts stereotypes. He scavenged discarded dresses, jackets, and market bags, refashioning them into new outfits, and dressing street-cast men in tight skirts, kimono gowns or in unconventional suits. Their ears, necks, and chests were festooned with costume jewellery and junk-shop brooches. His creations are distinctly African (Kamara hails from Sierra Leone and also has ties to Mali), but explore masculinity and menswear in a rule-free way, reawakening a thought-provoking conversation around gender presentation.

issues, engaging in personal and full-scale battles, with the aim of empowering this new generation, using arts, fashion, writing, social media and hashtags as a vehicle to spread the word and raise awareness all over.

The exciting pages of magazines, were invaded by young professionals, embracing their bold allure, and strong posture, trying to make a statement. It was such a kind of whirlwind of informations, a tumultuous anthem to the joy of experimenting, of asserting themselves and rewriting the social rules.

Garments were reinvented and reinterpreted in several ways and combinations, everyday objects added to catch the interest of the viewer, in an unconventional playful mix.

Ibrahim Kamara: in collaboration with photographer Kristin-Lee Moolman in, 2017; King Kong Magazine, Campbell Addy.

There was a sense of freedom, of respect for human beings.

After a long time dedicated to promote an unreal and disturbing ideal of "perfection", treacherously boosting people to abuse their bodies, punishing their natural variety, the fashion system was apparently moving into a safer, more intellectual direction, in which the individual was considered and emphasised in its fullness and complexity.

"Normal" people were center-stage, with their imperfections, aims, beliefs and emotional baggage that leaked out of their style.

The new generation of artists, photographers, designers, editors and so on, was completely embracing the whole "human experience" and translating it into powerful story-tellings.

Things were definitely changing, especially in fashion, turning it into a powerful vehicle, strong, engaging, conscious and young.

After all, garments without a purpose, a meaning and a story, will remain merely a nice piece of fabric, nothing more.

We were given the opportunity to refine, actually correct, the research process and the image collection, starting immediately after the break.

My classmates were on fire, googling "dramatic key words", with the aim of making a miracle happen, some others dedicated their efforts in the research of alumni's works, while me, I opted for some fresh new London magazines.

Persuaded by my obsolete love for printed paper and books, I pursued my personality, relying this time on a new-born sense of aesthetics, that hours of explanations, suggestions and critics, had re-designed or, I should say, at least encouraged.

The precious glimpses given, concerning different realities

and approaches, triggered something unexpected within our minds, a pervasive sense of curiosity. His speech, woke us up from a kind of mental lethargy. He chopped up us into pieces, ready to be spread all around in a huge universe of meanings, stories, different values, and then reconnected into several, diverse combinations.

We were all looking for something never considered before, all acting in unusual ways, far from the old patterns, out of our comfort zones, with our distinctiveness and uniqueness as the only companions.

The outcomes were undeniably great. I noticed the abyssal difference since the "first page scrolling" of my new journal. I identified key elements largely discussed during the tutorial, using a critical overture, being capable of providing reasons and explanations to myself for the choices made, and the type of selections conducted.

It was amazing!

Hidden in my decisions and perspective, a new personal taste, raw and more authentic, was progressively surfacing in me, I was coming into contact with my inner creative self, almost undisclosed.

Years of flatness had been ruthlessly eroding my intimate verve, my likings, numbing a persona who was still the middle of its growing process; this is the reason why, at a first glance, being left completely alone, without an "external guidance" to manage my own development, disoriented me, but then determined the occurrence of an unknown attitude to "problem-solving", and forced me to muster all of the precious skills and capabilities at my disposal.

I was curios and willing to apprehend.

I had to find my specific way to conduct the research, to

accomplish the task.

No one would have helped, nor channelled, me.

Rejecting a pedantic, conventional scheme, to push instead students to take control of their own learning, was the key strategy adopted by my University, resulting in one of the most effective and renowned in the world.

The progresses made trough a personal self evolution are the ones which can last long, forming a relevant inner part of the individuals themselves, whilst the use of external, strict patterns and schemes does not allow students to obtain the same level, considering that merely "accessing" is not "acquiring", and in order to deeply absorb something, an interiorisation process and a consistent effort are required, ensuring a subsequent advancement.

My pile was far less impressive in terms of quantity, compared to my previous research, but it delighted my tutors, due to the care involved in it.

We carried on with the selection of 10 types of faces, 20 poses and 10 fashion illustrations, moving progressively on to the next step.

The aim of this almost incomprehensible assignment, was setting the base for a future collection development, improving and implementing students' intellectual skills, while helping them to further develop existing capabilities, and channelling their creative personalities.

"Guys, I'll give you 2 minutes to draw a selected face or pose you like. No more! Are you ready?" Shouted Jack.

" 2 minutes ??" I thought. " It sounds like a joke!" I said, turning my face all around, looking for approvals among my

"Unfinished exercise": This represents the very first unsuccessful attempt of the drawing tutorial session. It shows a fashion pose, in which folds, and shadows, that a fabric naturally has as a consequence of the body movements, are emphasised.

The naturalistic way of reproducing every single detail, massively used for "observation drawings", resulted to be inadequate, "time-consuming" and impersonal, considering that the main focus was to pursue a type of unique interpretation of the pictures selected.

Despite the skills and capabilities involved in it, and my passionate and meticulous approach, the drawing did not lead me to accomplish the task.

On the contrary, it put the beginning of my performance in jeopardy.

peers.

I used to spend at least 1 hour on my drawings, enriching them with a clearly naturalistic approach, and a maniacal attention to details; having two minutes to complete that task was almost insane! Unfortunately there was no time for complaining, and I had to carry on with its execution."Stop!!" He thundered. Then he started again, again and again for several times, while at the end of each exercise, the result did not change a lot, our sheets were always partially empty.

After an unaccountable number of failing attempts, Jack started to sermonize, and we all had to stay in silence and feel the guilt of our "ineptitude".

" It's so damn pointless to stubbornly stick to observation drawings, when you have been given only 2 minutes. The idea was to reinterpret the image, not to photocopy it! I want you to be smart, fast and act in a resourceful way. I was expecting your personal version of the picture, not a banal copy! You will have 30 seconds more to complete this damn drawing! Go!"

Panic occurred. Drawing and erasing relentlessly, I lost my concentration, then I saw him coming to my desk, and I wanted to disappear completely.

"Hey, don't waste your time on this detail. Your are overthinking, Marella, stop caring, otherwise you'll end up with nothing. I'm going to show you a trick", he suggested, turning the picture sheet up-side down.

"How can I draw this way, Jack?" I genuinely reacted.

" You will! Concentrate on the lines, they'll guide you... and stop complaining!" he shouted.

Humbled, I went back to the design, dedicating my entire

"Final illustrations of the day": These 2 minutes drawings were obtained trough the use of different media, layered together.

The initial sketch was made with pencil, offering a guideline, on which to develop textures, proportion and colours, then a thin delicate layer with neutral Pantone, to recreate shadows.

The last phase involved the use of markers with different thicknesses, giving dynamism to the entire design.

attention to "its damn lines".

It seemed easier and far smoother. Blocks did not occur, nor hesitation.

When the timer rang, my drawing was almost complete.

What an incredible result!

Jack's suggestion of purely concentrating on the visual stimulus rather than the image in its wholeness, helped me overcoming my usual performance anxiety. The squared academical background I was still inflated with, that wanted me to be as precise and meticulous as hell, stopped my natural emotional flow, instead of fostering the flourishing of my individuality and ideas. That is why his action resulted in something kind of epiphanic, and so his drawing tutorial did.

The controlled exercise which had seemed so "banal and normal" at the beginning, secretly aimed to test and then provide an overview of our individualities, triggering a variety of reactions within the creative process, such as concerns, past education approach, blocks, fears, likings etc, while bringing them to the surface.

Jack was not only supposed to check the level of our outcomes that morning, if anything, he was discovering our selfhood, analysing inputs unconsciously provided.

He was collecting precious pieces of information about us, necessary for the tailored-made attitude, largely adopted in the School.

The University, was exactly like that: holding students' hands, conducting them into harsh routes, to stimulate a dialogue within their inner being, to then help the individual reconnect with their obsessions, memories, heritage, putting the base for a new creative sense, more genuine, more real, more passionate and definitely personal.

Training minds through ingenious yet simple exercises, demanding yet viable, was the beginning of a proper self discovery journey.

Students were center-stage. We, were center-stage. Everything was deeply revolving around us, and also depending on us.

A new sense of responsibility surfaced in me. The outstanding method enacted by our tutors, was indelibly shaping my way of thinking, whilst nurturing and urging my raw persona.

Being given the freedom of self-conducting my progression, plus a constant "confidence injection" with the reassuring motto: "hard work beats talent, when talent does not work", clearly referred to the prominent role of commitment and will power, channelled me to both a more conscious creative dimension and a more adult size.

After all, creativity, although it refers to the natural way people think, it is also influenced by two other essential factors, such as expertise and, most of all, motivation, "intrinsic motivation" (completely missing in me throughout my previous experiences).

Hence, it appears fundamental to encourage individuals, in this case students, to nurture their peculiarities and certain levels of engagement within their work, rather than suppress them. "Intrinsic motivation", in particular, is the key ingredient, which could be spurred by adopting effective training strategies, or conversely seriously compromised, inevitably affecting the imaginative growth. It drives people to reach outstanding and, often, innovative outcomes, but if there is a lack in terms of commitment and genuine passion, despite the great educational credentials and facility in generating new perspectives, they will either not accomplish it or simply stick to old-fashioned, obsolete schemes, without really producing newness.[8]

The London University, totally encompassed this type of "intrinsic motivation" concerning teaching methodologies, considering it as a "key strategy" to "crack problems" with more innovative solutions, that no one else had been able to solve, and to produce a sentiment of fullness and satisfaction within students, whilst addressing them to a deep self-understanding. Their tasks were motivating themselves, in order to guarantee a high level of engagement, of challenge and enjoyment, during all of the phases involved.

On the contrary, in a traditional academical environment, the tendency largely embraced in fostering the individual motivation, is mostly based on the adoption of external factors, producing a sort of negative pressure, which clearly will not guarantee a real engagement, nor the flourishing of ideas and creative thinking. This sort of motivation called "extrinsic", makes people do the job in order to get something desirable and avoid something painful, leading them to feel as if they are being bribed and controlled, and affecting their self esteem and psychic health.

Extrinsic motivation, cannot make somebody passionate about a job, nor cope with the limitations provided by its own nature.

By contrast, interest, satisfaction, autonomy and responsibility, trigger individual creativity more than external

---

[8]   Teresa Amabile, "How to kill creativity", *Harvard Business Review.*

pressure, stretching and stimulating the expertise, skills and imaginative thinking in a balanced way. People need to feel free, in order to push their boundaries, and heighten their intrinsic motivation and sense of ownership, making the most out of themselves.

At the end of the day, we all experienced a sense of fullness, confidence and desire to succeed.

The complexity of the process, hidden in apparent simple assignments, not only did help us to canvass and test our potential, but also gave us the possibility of developing a fresh new expertise and vision in terms of drawing.

Unexpectedly, after multiple controlled exercises, we matured a considerable speed in analysing pictures and lines, plus a deep awareness of what was relevant for each of us, producing more personal outcomes in which distinctive skills, perspectives and tastes predominated.

Once finished our class, we were all able to draw a face, a fashion pose and illustration in approximately two minutes, while maintaining naturally heterogeneous levels of designs.

The purpose was not just to speed up students' drawing skills, but most importantly, digging out their "persona and uniqueness", whilst helping them to keep up in a professional, highly competitive environment such as fashion.

It was the beginning of a journey, the foundations of the creative process, sought to channel students towards their specific area of interests, and to assist them during the acknowledgement and understanding of a variety of important elements involved in it.

Tutors were accompanying us trough a series of "mechanical exercises", designed to enhance our verve from the basics, to build a solid mindset and to create an established method of processing ideas, on an individual basis.

We spent the following weeks, working primarily on images interpretation, collages and personal style, already trained to quick sketches, and we were encouraged to move forward onto a more imaginative unusual dimension.

The idea of making "collages", often linked to childish plays, became the core of the first term of the course, obviously unleashing a wider sense of curiosity and interest among me and my peers.

First, had come the studio of human body and faces etc., then its relative pose and proportion, and now, it was the turn of collages and compositions.

We were all wondering about its importance, unknowingly undervaluing the evocative power that a very manual and visual exercise could have.

The aim was to be exposed to a basic play, made of several material pieces, of colourful inputs, to encourage our visionary skills in producing meta-realities, subverting the natural order of things, and exploring our aesthetics.

We started early on a Monday morning to sketch a minimum of human figures, that would have been filled and covered at a second time with sheets scraps, pieces of paper, and so on, in order to start the empowering process of collaging.

We should have found interesting combinations of patterns and silhouettes, paying attention to their level of complexity and sophistication. The use of existing garments was not allowed, and so they were surreal compositions leaving aside fashion aspects and components.

Meanwhile, the real, serious problem within myself , was

represented by the "ancient envy" nurtured and felt for the "making of collages".

Additionally, I used to get lost when exposed to "infinite possibilities", so that catching attractive features within several images, was more than a torture to me.

"Such a great start. I have to get these illustrations done, the faster the better." I thought.

I had to find a way to cope with this intimate sense of disappointment, take a deep breath and work on this task as quickly as possible.

I decided to start from three brand new magazines I had purchased in the morning (as it always happened). Before doing this, I had had a look all around, noticing that my peers were gloriously busy with their research and images collections; some were focusing on colours, patterns, others on artworks and abstract things, I was the old-paper lover, scrolling magazines.

I marked every meaningful page, once analysed its content, with post-its, different colours for different uses, such as: the reds stood for shape, greens for objects, yellows for patterns and so on, in order to maintain a fluid procedure trough the simple scrolling on pages.

At the beginning I felt overwhelmed by the vast amount of data, too much of everything, and the more I looked at them, the more I lost any idea of where to start from.

It was a kind of a loop.

The initial attempts, resulted in picturesque figures, bulky, gross and obsolete, portraying respectively the mythological Medusa, and the Flintstones... and...

Can you imagine who came to visit me, in that very moment?

Any ideas???

Obviously, Jack.

I was ready for his imminent outburst, considering the ridiculous outcome, but he showed a calm and unexpectedly nice attitude and, snatching the sheets, he started the one to one session with me.

"Marella, can you please explain to me what this is? I mean, these illustrations look clearly as a piece of crap!"

"Oh, here you go man! It was too good to be true, too calm and polite to be you", I thought, already prepared to his "sophisticated manners".

But anyway, I could not escape the crit, and I had to motivate and give a reason to what I had been doing thus far and....

" Well, yes, I agree, as you can see, there are here two massive pieces of crap I need to work on" I replied, trying to enjoy this new "intellectual" approach.

"Ok then, you got it! I'll be back, please try to amaze me!"

He was rude, abusive and poisonous, but his suggestions were so damn excellent.

He mocked me, and in a way intimidated me, while enlightening my critical and creative sense.

The lecture received, persuaded me to adopt a depth I was not likely to use, searching for answers within myself.

His manners and behaviours pushed me to go outside of my comfort-zone, something undeniably useful and fruitful for my inner growth.

He woke me up from my numbness, providing the will and strength to start again, and prove myself I was worth more than a first try.

He helped me a lot.

Undefined "Mythological figures": These collages show all the limitations in terms of appeal, that arise from a too literal approach. Despite their vivid colours and textures, that tended to unhinge and intrigue a viewer, at a first glance, the massive presence of fashionable elements, combined with too many fancy pieces, stuck on garments, results in a very heavy and gross composition, which clearly did not match neither the briefing nor my tutors' expectations. There was no variety in terms of shape, nor unusual elements, apart from the banal use of prints, mixed and layered together following a "pretty-nice-pattern"

Contemplating my "archaic characters", I scanned every details in desperate need for noticing "the missing part", the "wrong element", and after a long hour of silent dialogue, I spotted the key problem which had jeopardized the entire assignment.

What really had compromised my illustrations, was the anxious approach which drove me to adopt banal solutions, such as garments pieces already arranged, instead of displaying and figuring a personal world of choices and symbols.

A radical change was necessary to feel the gap, in terms of "information selection".

I had to start again, this time with a a proactive and positive attitude, clearing up all sort of concerns and constraints, giving myself a dimension of playful autonomy. After all it was a collage, not a military campaign.

I started to dwell on images, elements and colours to detect what was "honestly" attracting me, dividing the creative process in two parts.

The starting point was represented by a thorough material research, this time mainly focusing on the pure visual stimulus, matching my personality and mind rather than my purpose.The new overture, completely detached from the "pervasive idea of fashion", helped me to stay open, pursuing an happier yet honest direction, allowing likings, personal tastes, preferences guided me in the "cutting process".

Finally, my selection appeared far different compared to the beginning and incredibly multifaceted, both in terms of shape, proportions and references.

I was then ready to start the second part, with all this vivid material at my disposal, it was the moment of concentrating on clothes silhouettes and composition. There was no order, nor a pattern, I just followed the flow, being inspired by colours and forms, their evocative power, visual ideas, and whilst moving, layering and changing them, the collages took shape.

At the end of the day, I proudly showed my ten new "babies" to the tutor, detecting a hidden smile of approval, not for the design themselves, but for the lesson learnt, for the passionate commitment that pushed me outside the lines, to perfect my work.

What the School had taught me thus far, was that "failure" is a key ingredient, almost essential, for innovation.

So that, not every proposal of change can be successful, as in my case, some of them failed, but always providing a "potential truth", which is essential for future goals achievement.

My tutors were all embracing a new and outstanding philosophy completely focused on rehabilitating the importance of failure, prone to stimulate creativity by encouraging students to risk in a kind of "safe environment", or should I say, giving them some limits.

This is approach is also known as "Intelligent fast failure".

The purpose is to move as quickly as possible from new ideas to new knowledge by making small and manageable mistakes (intelligent failure) along the way of a multitude of attempts. Letting students to be independent enough to guide their personal failing, and perfect their own processes, while being channelled by some quick suggestion as external limit.

To better understand how and why "crashes" are considered as useful as sometimes fundamental in a creative growing path, to improve experience and innovative outcomes, it is

"Final collages": Any difference?

necessary to simply reflect on a bird's nest construction:

"The bird collects twigs and place them on a small ledge. The wind blows some of the twigs away. The bird sees this, and brings in larger twigs. A rainstorm washes some twigs away. The bird replaces those with heavier twigs Eventually the nest is built."

For the bird each issue was part of the process, of the journey itself, not a "proper failure", as all humans are likely to consider it. Each failure provided a partial truth, so when sufficient knowledge was acquired, the bird is able to build a long lasting nest. And so we are, and so my collages eventually *would have been.*[9]

Months were passing by so fast, tasks were becoming more and more difficult, and so, our expertise and capabilities, were growing accordingly.

After the intense period dedicated to training our minds, and reshape and enhance the creative approach, with a new sense of awareness and autonomy, concerning also the management of our key strengths and weaknesses, we were all ready to start a long lasting journey towards fashion's real core, such as the "making of a collection".

It should have been something really original, unusual and unique, driven by the inside part of ourselves, our raw persona. A perfect combination of our peculiar ways of translating reality, a distinctive investigation and interpretation of the environments around us, both concrete and imaginative.

According to this purpose, the collage-task given became a "bridge", connecting the "exploration-phase" with the "development-stage"; we had to draw a precise copy of them, taking into account every details, creating a proper illustration, then we focused on a colour palette, which could have matched them all, giving to the "line-up" (selected look within a collection), a sense of coherency and consistency. Shapes and form which were too abstract, were studied with accuracy and translated into proper garment parts, shoes and accessories were added, as well as a simple concept to refer to for colours and fabrics involved.

And actually the collection took form, the first very unitary project.

---

[9]   Dr. Jack Matson "The role of fast failure in driving innovation" On-line article 2014 by Lisa Fuchs.

The first term, ended with this surprising book, containing in a way, all our efforts, changes, improvements and natural diversity.

The tutors, brought out our raw material, subverting habits, concerns and fears.

In a very small portion of time, my beliefs, methods and perspectives changed dramatically, I was as a "river in flood", full of flourishing ideas, a new sense of awareness, a more mature understanding on what fashion really represented to me, with a newfound confidence. My final project, appeared miles away from the standard, commercial feminine clothes I worked on for half of my existence; the new proposals looked big, unconventional, weird and definitely more detailed and real, and luckily they enabled me to pass the final evaluation test at the end of the first module, letting me advance to the second part of the course.

After the "assessment" session, the ones with a positive feed-back automatically shifted to the higher level, while the others were dismissed.

We were given two months break, for summer holidays, to then start at the beginning of September.

Faces: Designs produced trough a controlled exercise,
from a minimum of 1 minute to 5 minutes, using different media, such us pen, pencil, watercolour and markers.

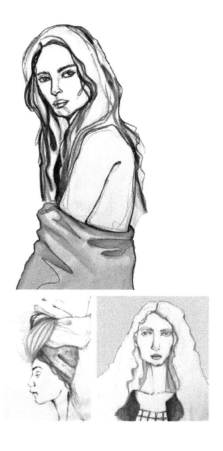

Faces: Designs produced trough a controlled exercise, from a minimum of 1 minute to 5 minutes, using different media, such us pen, pencil, watercolour and markers.

Fashion illustrations: Techniques involved: Pencil
on markers, photoshop, pen and watercolour
(From 2 minutes to 15 minutes)

CHAPTER FIVE

From a blank canvas to garments:

Creative process through sketches, inspiration, attempts, dramas and self-understanding.

In order to be gratified by your own creative outcomes, three key ingredients are absolutely necessary: Honesty, inquisitive mind and a strong critical sense.

Every designer tends to be influenced by their heritage and personality in every step of their work, so that reaching a deep level of understanding their distinctive spots and exploring their own persona, represents the base of every imaginative and creative process, to then consequently adopt a honest direction into the research and development phase.

What I had learnt thus far was to assume that you are guiding your own progression and growth, the crucial role that ideas play within a project, and the inspirational elements that trigger them.

Inputs, visual stimulus etc. need to be carefully and "honestly" selected, considering their inner capacity of thrilling our verve and imagination, that depends essentially on the hidden connections they have with our deepest parts, and the strong influence to either arouse or shut down our mental excitement, engagement and interest.

I experienced first hand the importance of not only adopting personal methods, but also materials, concepts and things with a clear evocative power or, I should say, that "can speak to you", in order to avoid a "dead-end" that otherwise might occur even after considerable efforts.

After all, if an idea does not awake your senses and perceptions, it simply does not work for you. If it cannot provide enlightenment, emotions and fruitful feelings, it is predictable it will cause a kind of distancing from your purpose and work, rather than engagement. Try not to lie to yourself, it would be time consuming, giving rise to unproductive situations.

It is always advisable to stop for questioning whether something is appropriate or not, respondent and meaningful to you, and if necessary go a few steps back to restore some balance.

Generally, things and connections involved in a project are likely to change along the way, experimentations, corrections and so on, are essential to then define "what your work will be all about", and the necessary techniques and skills to apply.

Creative processes, in fact, are strongly related to the natural organisation of our minds, so the best option is to steer into it, and let your sense select key elements to explore and develop, rather than plan since the very beginning every detail of your process, which may affect the fluency and spontaneity of it.

The inner, raw material within each individual, needs to be implicated and used, representing the richest tank of creativity.

If adopting a "honest approach" might be considered as a part of a self-discovery process, on the other hand, maturing a critical sense and inquisitive mind, then constitutes a relevant portion of a designer expertise, which can be fostered and fed externally.

The condition of "being inquisitive" is natural in some individuals, driven by their incessant curiosity and sophisticated approach to life, prone to investigate in depth relevant elements with a sharp eye for details and the will of catching the inner meaning of things.

Being inquisitive is something that could also be built day by day, by enriching and immersing ourselves in a multitude of realities and stimuli, while training the brain to select pieces of information that urge to be questioned and further explored, which is in a way connects to the "critical sense".

The ability of going into something, is often an intelligent mind's prerogative, especially if the "etymological origin" of the word "intelligence" is taken into account, which clearly shows its link to the ancient Latin language.

The verb "intellego", arises from the union of the Latin adverb "intus", that means inside, and the verb "lego", which is strongly related to the idea of "reading, understanding, collecting ideas", so it appears obvious that being intelligent could be explained as an attitude of some human beings of "going in depth into things", exploring the reality while collecting and connecting to its hidden gems and aspects, hardly understandable.

While commonly accounted to bright minds, critical sense, on the contrary, happens to not always be a natural born gift, just like talent does not, too, after all. It represents the third essential ingredient to advance in every creative process, while maintaining decent levels of satisfaction and self-growth.

Showing a critical and open-minded approach is a life long process, in some cases kind of complex and tough. Being critical means putting our natural mental bias to the test, constantly, without exceeding with counterproductive overtures.

It means being capable of evaluating with "honesty" our selves, outcomes and so on, aiming to learn and push the boundaries of knowledge.

The word "critical", may also suggest a negative aspect, as many individuals tend to undeniably reconnect it to adverse situations or a judgemental dimension, which can be seen as a kind of contradiction in terms, if we consider that the capability of questioning, analysing, conceptualizing, evaluating and then understanding, happens to be more than a positive attitude.

This condition in processing data would be idyllic. Unfortunately, though, humans pass over the initial steps, reaching too early the "dangerous"phase of "evaluation, completely missing a precious logical approach that would led to the right conclusions and ending up with "mental shortcuts" instead, often called "heuristics".

These "heuristics" are a natural and innate brain's tendency that occurs in making decisions, or answering questions, and it is based on "fast intuitive connections".

"As logical as we think we are, our brain deals better with intuition than logic, with generalization rather than statistics, and generally the brain's failure to apply logical rules and its tendency to use heuristics can jeopardize our performance, understanding and outcomes." [10]

According to this, humans are not spontaneously capable of facing and benefitting from a huge variety of possibilities, without using their experiences, tastes and personalities, unconsciously losing a logical perspective, inscribing things into limits and barriers.

Our minds are keen to label everything they process, that is why maturing a critical sense is something that needs to be constantly fed and nurtured with a genuine eye-opened to the unknown, unpredictable, not perfected world.

---

[10]   College info Geek " Want to think better? Avoid these six cognitive bias" Ransom Patterson 2015.

"Thinking is skilled work. It is not true that we are naturally endowed with the ability to think clearly and logically, without learning out and practicing". [11]

Cognitive bias and illusions will always be there, in our brain, ready to jump out, so it depends on our deliberate choice whether to follow them or to try and adopt a reasoned, impartial overture in our existence and projects.

Since the beginning of the second term, we were introduced to the core of the real creative process, this time without the aid of any controlled exercise.

Luckily, we had been addressed to the new, direct approach through a summer task, assigned before the end of the course term.

At a first glance, the "homework", seemed to be pretty relaxing and enjoyable, being focused on the production of several "sketch-books", with high levels of autonomy.

No one had a clear idea of what to represent on it, nor the role and importance played by them, so that our tutors decided to concentrate all the tutorials on this specific, crucial topic.

This "hand-made art diary" appeared to have a mythological or sacred origin; when on a desk, all the tutors tended to religiously move all around the corner to form a kind of circle, with their eyes firmly opened and directed to the small piles of sheets, "from which you can see amazing, and intriguing things coming out the edges" they used to say.

They were completely gone.

The leader of the the program, in particular, was kind of obsessed with "booklets", amused, pleased and delighted by their only view, never failed to show us his extreme

---

[11]   A.E. Mander.

attachment, each time, through hilarious behaviours.

He had a type of ritual in approaching them, made of different phases.

First, he had to sit on a chair, finding a comfortable position for approximately 30 seconds, moving and adjusting his jersey jacket, then he put the "sketch-book"on the desk, right in front of his hands and visual area, so that it could not have escaped.

After that, the crucial part, represented by the overture of the first page: you might have seen him reaching a peak of pleasure, he was on fire, handling the book with uncountable care, caressing and appreciating every single part of the pages.

He was literally having an orgasm.

This procedure generally lasted for 10 minutes, before the start of the proper tutorial, the director all immersed in the "appreciation process" basically used to forget we were all waiting for the the lesson to start.

He needed to be absent, dwelling and indulging in frills, pieces of fabrics and illustration that were coming out from the rhythmic scrolling of the pages, he urged that small portion of time to abstract himself from the everyday reality, or maybe "we" were just less interesting and intriguing than the sketch-book.

Before that moment, I had never heard about the existence of a sketch-book, or I should say, for sure, not in these terms.

Years before, during my work experiences at the company, I used to keep a diary for my daily activities, such as material selections, notes, collection drafts and so on, which resembled more of an agenda than a proper inspirational booklet.

The pages were clean and organized, written notes all over, while both the creative and personal sign were almost absent,

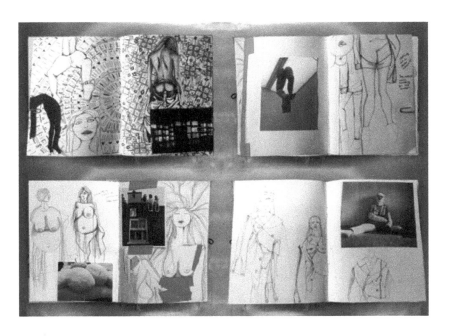

Sketch-books examples: The picture shows four different types of sketch-book, produced over 4 months. Some of them (two) are directly connected, and belonged to the winter project I developed during the second term, others are just parts of a personal area of research and interest.

apart from my maniacal obsession with order.

It was an aseptic, well-planned diary, that showed no traces of unique artistic touch, nor a distinguishable personality, it could have possibly belonged to anyone else.

On the contrary, the works displayed during the tutorials, were full of information, almost exploding by the quantity of ideas, references and research stuffed in them.

"Sketch-books" attractiveness was due to the spontaneous care used in placing images, drawings and drafts, beautifully made and reasoned, preserving a clear sense of personality, distinctiveness and uniqueness, thanks to the use of some peculiar techniques included in them.

"Sketch-books", indeed, represent a kind of window into the artists soul, aims, perspectives and beliefs, offering insights and glimpses of their imaginative reality, showing undisclosed processes and a visual explanation of the ideas development. So it appears fundamental to have them real and personal, unique and recognisable, containing raw materials, experimentations, doodles, failing attempts and several techniques. It is almost impossible and futile to keep them tidy and clean, but advisable to make them interesting and creatively organized, in order to also communicate a sense of professionalism in showing them, when required.

As our director kept on saying, they are an artist/designer's everyday diary, that needs to be consumed, enlarged and expanded with new sheets, collecting and reflecting everything that attracts and thrills the imaginative verve.

A booklet can be the starting point for the research area you are focusing on, or merely a physical support on which to pin some great ideas to be better explored.

I had to start immediately this new sketch-book, giving it a chance, and a completely new dimension and taste, miles away from my controlled tendency to perfectionism and tidiness.

I approached timidly the first page, at the beginning of my summer holidays, slightly suffering from the "white-page-crisis".

The first few days, I discovered myself contemplating the small A5 booklet (my favourite format), almost empty, staying right in front of me on the desk.

I kept on questioning what to include, subjects and references to start with, and...

"What the hell am I doing, sitting like a fool, trying to organize my personal diary! Not an academical paper, but a diary, god!! It should have been so natural and spontaneous! So, now Marella , don't overthink, don't make plans, don't be obsessed with your sense of order, and please get this s#!* done".

Hours were passing by, and I was too full and empty at the same time, unconsciously engrossed in a variety of data that were moving incessantly in my head. This first ever sketch-book, was giving me a really hard time; but as it is often the case, when a solution is not easily found on the right side, it is convenient to subvert it, upside down.

With a critical sense by my side, I directed my attention to intimate needs and necessities I felt, in order to let my creative verve flourish; indeed, it was not my brain which was not collaborating, but the condition I was trying to force it in, that actually was not triggering any results nor excitement in it.

I was alone in my small room, sitting on the desk, how could have I thrilled myself in that occasion?

I urged stimulus, visual inputs and ideas. I needed to go out, see the world out there, reflect, collect and immerse myself. And then, again.

The external aid did the work, and once discovered amazing spots close to my apartment, before I knew it, the flow of my thoughts conducted me to the Tate Modern, which I am so passionate about.

Museums contributed and still contribute to the preliminary phase of every creative process, representing a crucial and consistent part of my topics exploration.

I have always felt inspired by art, in general, having a specific "fetish" for modern and contemporary paintings, photography, installations and fiber-art. That is the reason why, in that case, I spontaneously drove myself to the Tate, without even questioning it.

1 Hour later

At the Tate Modern, everything excited my creative verve, its location and internal structure were paradisiacal, without mentioning the precious artistic component, hidden within its strong walls.

I took several pictures in the basement, then I moved trough the concrete stairs of the Switch House, reaching the upper floors. I passed the permanent collection, craving for something new that could have awoken my senses; walking around, I found a lateral entrance of a small little room, that seemed to host a temporary exhibition.

I decided to ask for some more information at a desk, standing on the left hand side of the entrance, trying to show the most sophisticated attitude I have ever had, as if I were an art critic; but, in the first 30 seconds I immediately embarrassed myself.

I asked for the name of the artist, without even noticing the label was just in front of the door, and when realized it, I could not have read it properly due to my incessant myopia and my ridiculous habit of not using glasses. Then, I tried to restore my dignity somehow, talking about the artist, about its talent and the importance of exhibiting not only well-known artist but also some niche.

Epic fail!

Not only did I lie, imperiously talking about somebody I completely ignored, but also making a miserable mistake, asserting she (The artist) belonged to a niche, when, on the contrary, she was world renowned.

"Marella, it's time to go, please, shut up" I said to myself, after the awkward episode.

The lateral small room, partially dark, was occupied in the middle by a long rectangular crate, all transparent, made in perspex; inside it, unusual soft sculptures, resembling circular breasts, pink and soft, filled with foam (I supposed), were laid in an apparent messy order, similar to a mushrooms colony over a tree trunk.

They tucked my interest, at first sight. My mind was already creating secret intuitive and evocative connections, something hidden within those artworks triggered a deep relation between me and the amazing artist, Louise Bourgeois.

The hairy texture of the "breast-pillows", thrilled my imaginary, made of women's nudity, fluent femininity and a clear obsession for researching a sense of absolute harmony and wholeness within a body.

I filled my first page, scribbling this kind of breasts in a red colour shade.

After half an hour, partially aloof from reality, I entered the second, and actually the main room of the exhibition, discovering the most powerful yet distressing example of vivid emotions, as well as a dramatic attempt of establishing a harmoniously ordered totality of structural relationship. [12]

I met "*maman*", the imperious, metal spider, the artist created referring to the only stable liaison she had in her life.

The sculpture was powerful, immense, touching the wall, bony and knobby, as an ancient tree, dark and resistant, as only an eternal, frayed maternal bond could be.

Deep, amazing and disturbing.

I felt the necessity of crying, I was overwhelmed, and surrounded by its beauty and depth, by this absolute time of remembrance, of a woman fighting over her inner self. The symbolic components were exhibiting her past experiences, pain and childish parts, vivid and imbued with grief.

My internal conflicts, and memories started to melt.

Not only *maman*, but also a *cage*, impressive *paintings, red fabric legs* hung as a cluster on the ceiling, and so on, were all starring at me.

It seemed an oneiric scene, with apparently disconnected and diverse elements, an "illusionary circus of dead thoughts, of past experiences and living feelings".

The flow of my thoughts was channelling me into a very unexpected dimension, reconnecting my soul to an undisclosed tank of emotions.

I was drawing relentlessly, mixing and interpreting the artworks with imaginative subjects.

---

[12]   David Bohm "On creativity" page 27.

I was trusting just my own vibes, letting my inner energy flush on the paper, without being completely conscious about the direction to follow, the areas to explore.

One thing was pretty clear to me: the importance and consequent impact that relationships have in human existence, would have been my new subject of research, as well as their inner capability of influencing our condition, our lives, triggering unusual reactions and emotions.

"A sense of fragmentation, emptiness and precariety, within our existence, are hardly understandable among humans, becoming one of the essential illness we are suffering today.

The response to this phenomenon is probably to be found, considering the individual psychological need of establishing such an harmonious and whole totality of "structural relationships", in order to assimilate all of the experiences, both of the external environment and his internal psychological processes.

When, this hypothetical state of fullness and fulfilment is not reached, some of the experiences not properly digested start to work as a "virus", producing an ever growing state of disharmony and conflicts, which leads to destroy and numb a man's mind.

Such as in this case, which concerns the artist.

That sense of pain, spread all over the exhibition main room, displayed at its best and most vivid accent, was nothing less then the author's magnificent attempt to cope with such a load of emotions and internal struggles in the field of self-knowledge.

Art, indeed, entered this delicate area, providing a kind of symbolism, expressing as a proper vehicle, the artist's state of confusion and uncertainty, acting in the hope that giving visible shape to disease can somehow trigger a mastery over them.

Positive feelings often related to the "work of art", are unlikely based on illusions, determining a kind of self-induced circle in which a temporary phase of satisfaction, gradually moves to a new conflicted and disturbed one.

On the contrary, the proper way to deal with conflict, is to look at it directly by being aware of the full meaning of what one is doing and thinking. As the artist herself said about the importance of self-understanding and learning [13] :"You learn for yourself not for others, not to show off, not to put the other down. Learning is your secret, it is all you have, it is the only thing you can call your own. Nobody can take it away [...]" [14]

Accordingly, the role of art, is to teach the artistic spirit of a "sensitive perception" of the individual and particular phenomena of one's own psyche. As long as it is provided oneself a sense of understanding within things, and assimilated it, individuals will feel at home.

"Once, I was beset by anxiety, but I pushed the fear away by studying the sky, determining when the moon would have come out". [15]

Meanwhile, engrossed in my deep thoughts, I drew a long, thin, vivid line. A red line, halving the page. Then I made a second, a third and so on.

The page was metaphorically slashed by these pencil signs, which were the visual representation of human relations and interactions, outstretched towards something, with a start and

---

[13]   David Bohm "On creativity" page 27

[14]   Louise Bourgeois "The return of the repressed"- Psychoanalytical writings

[15]   Louise Bourgeois

an end, amazingly soft and terribly rigid when in pressure.

Sometimes hung.

Sometimes interrupted. Humans.

In my mind they were the ultimate vehicle of voicing our stories, connecting and distancing people's emotions.

The day spent at the Tate modern, was kind of epiphanic; with a precarious mental condition, and memories and experiences partially deconstructed, I finally felt the need of exploring and reshaping myself.

I arrived at home late that night, shaken, worn out and terribly excited.

I could have not believed the creative phase might have been so spontaneous.

I felt in the throes of working, studying, investigating and experimenting. My sketch-book was almost full, my brain processes were placed all over, drawings, notes, scribbles and so on. The theme of my exploration, not yet clearly defined, religiously followed my silent impulse and experience, taking form progressively.

It would have been possible to notice and detect a rhythmic evolution of the concept, trough the scrolling of pages, everything was unconsciously and mentally connected, on a soulful level. There was this silent dialogue between me and this "undefined" project, which was containing all of my distinctive information, such as "maman" was doing with Louise Bourgeois (even though on a different artistic level).

I worked almost all night, completely absorbed and obsessed by the idea of letting the unknown part of my "persona" surface through the creative process.

At 3 o' clock, deprived by every type of human stimulus, I decided to give myself a break, for a couple of hours.

However, the material collected thus far, was largely focused on artworks, and so were the accountable number of interpretations and cues of it, there was almost no presence of fashion elements, nor any applications.

The following day, I would have had to move one step back, to fill the gap, introducing "the thread idea" on a more material level, looking for fabrics to manipulate.

After all, I was trying to become a fashion designer, I could have not skipped the "essential phase" of producing newness trough hundreds of manual and conceptual failing attempts.

End of the holidays, three weeks later

Trusting my own vibes, senses and intuitive capacity, I had produced a considerable amount of work, without being channeled by anyone, concerning the approach to use during a sketch-book-project development.

The garment exploration, which, in the past, generally moved on a more aesthetic level, in this case became saturated with meaning. In my spontaneous growing, the process was guiding itself, pushing into different directions, finding connections, and relating several subjects to a deeper level. At some point, I found myself completely changed.

Despite the visible changes, within my imaginative and practical approach, some illustrations provided by my incessant research, needed to be conceptualized and aligned to that "complex affair", and definitely merged into a "newfound personal voice".

The course leader was right when obsessively insisting on the importance of using an artistic diary, not only for building ideas but also for improving on a more personal level.

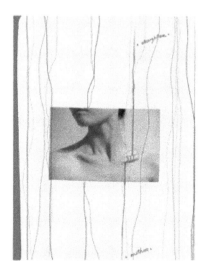

Sketch-book cover: It represents the beginning of the "Thread project", through the exploration of the interruption of a maternal bond. The research conducted, involved different types of techniques, such as collages, drawing on pictures to better extend and communicate aims and objectives, and to create a personal and distinctive interpretation of the concept itself.

The solo-procedure, made of lonely hours spent with delicate and passionate introspective drawings, manual works, had led me to better understand what really triggered and thrilled my verve, within a research.

My priority, although I was still operating on a partially unconscious dimension, was "using fashion and visual research as a vehicle of my inner voice". I felt as if I had the

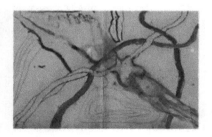

Sketch-book page: The main giant focus, was represented by the frailty of the "bond among mother and daughter", with its subsequent interruption and the collateral and related themes-reactions arose.

The red threads symbolized at their best, the fatigue, and misery due to its premature separation.

dramatic urgency of speaking out loud, analysing, connecting and shouting what "I" was really about.

Once immersed in that weighty scenery at the Tate, an internal energy , that had been silently resting for so many years, started its whirlwind endless movement, convulsively waving in me. I could not stop hearing its chaotic noise, I had difficulties to properly isolate a single sound, emotion, thought. It was dancing and moving rapidly, creating curlicues, ripples, waiting to desperately come out.

Louise Bourgeois's work, indeed, played a crucial role, and had a very strong influence and impact on me, determining a surprising openness on a soulful level, thus being exposed without psychological barriers and bias to the tough reality of "her painful life", awoken something within my psyche, channeling me into an unplanned psychological condition of nudity.

It was the time to deeply plunge into my real being, hopefully finding a guideline to follow for my creative process, aware that pain, memories and undisclosed thoughts would have been all sitting over there, in the dark, some with a positive attitude, some others as hungry creatures.

I would not have digested my own discovery easily, but the growing and imaginative process also passes through honesty.

My first attempt concerning "the selection phase" of the threads, happened to be incomplete, conceptual and still partial, due to the only usage of illustrations and collages. I needed to translate the raw ideas into something visible, touchable, searching both an appropriate material and size to start my experimentation.

After several inconclusive days spent in fabric shops, I finally found a very thin wool skein, soft, bright and slightly hairy, in a deep shade of red, enough to impress a viewer; the main concern remained "how to use it, and how to effectively translate the flood of emotions through a manual work".

With the inspiring, obsessive and captivating idea of the "red thread" in my mind, I felt enlightened and I started to draft interesting garment applications and techniques with "my babe" center-stage.

The most attractive option was a textile completely made of thin threads, invisibly attached, maintaining a sense of softness and flexibility. In relation to this, the challenge was represented by the tools and techniques to adopt in order to obtain the desired effect.

After several tests, with every type of glue, ended in such a dead-end, I opted for an unusual solution, hoping for the best.

Once cut the threads with a length of approximately two metres, I laid them vertically, and started to sprinkle them with the "strongest hair-spray" on the market, having care of the edges, holes in between, the hairy surface and so on; then I left them for two hours, occasionally checking their status.

This procedure lasted for 3-4 days, before I noticed an initial result.

Out of my expectations, the apparently weak hair fixer, after layers of patient exposure, created a very strong bond, almost invisible, but soft, manageable and flexible.

I could not believe my eyes, the single thin threads were, now, an impressive red parade.

I was proud of the result achieved, and with this "heirloom" beside me, I felt ready to start the second term of the course.

Sometimes the learning process and self growth, can also pass unnoticed, without a period of what is generally deemed as a "conventional training".

The trick of the "easy-going" task was exactly this, letting us free and alone, in guiding the progression of our own expertise and creative advancement.

Without preconceived patters and paths to follow, I forced myself in finding solutions, testing unknown approaches and techniques, discovering new tools, common and uncommon, expanding my knowledge, improving my critical sense and my artistic resourcefulness, unconsciously setting up a proper work-process.

My "solo-studies"taught me how to properly conduct a conceptual research, collecting visual materials, stimuli and how to adapt them on a meaningful basis, developing a coherent and consistent concept.

Reasonably enough, I did not have the mastery of it yet, but at least I started to unconsciously benefit from this new methodology and sense of autonomy.

Beginning of the "Second Term"

The first few days, passed by slowly, people seemed all numbed by the time off.

Tutors, conducted a preliminary check among our booklets, suggesting different procedures and timings for each of us, according to the progresses made and quantity of work.

Before the actual start of the classes, we were divided into several groups, each by the course we were aiming to apply for.

I was moved into the small room, with a couple of peers,

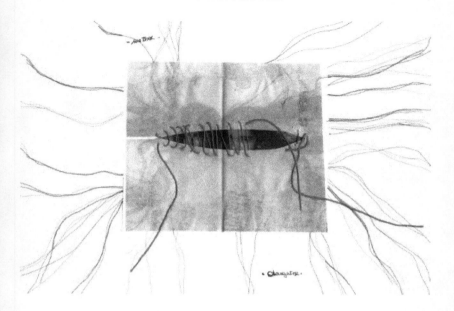

and as future post-graduate students, we would have been exposed to different levels of difficulties and complexities. The ones applying for the BA, on the contrary, stayed in the previous beloved location.

My new place, silent and secluded, immediately became a flourishing source of inspiration.

There was no crowd, nor noise, we were just six students, religiously working on our projects.

It was a heaven!

My desk was at the end of the room, backed on the wall, very long, with a rectangular shape, giving me the possibility of organizing my work-station in sectors: on the left part, more external, catching immediately the people's view, I decided to lay my experimentations out, while sketch-books and parts in progress were piled in the middle and right hand side, well hidden.

As I was expecting, my organization, produced the aimed result; tutors entered the room, and seemed attracted by the "long expanse of red", even if with a clear sign of interest and approval, they left me alone, progressing with the project.

At some point of the research and concept development, I had the necessity of beginning the stand-studies, the drawing phase was likely to go in a dangerous loop, so it appeared crucial to start the practical application, not only concerning the textile, but also the draping, in order to explore shapes

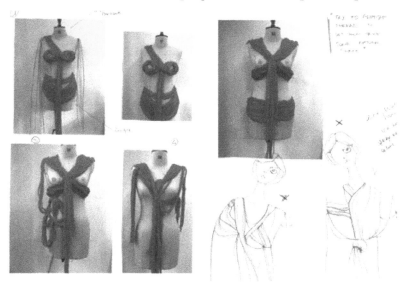

"Threads project" draping: As it is clear in the picture, the silhouettes created, resulted in a meaningless bulky shape. The page is part of one of the sketch-books, largely used for the design and draping phase. Notes, scribbles and marks, are vital for the selection and ideas elaboration, showing also a creative approach and method distinctively personal.

and silhouettes

Once chosen a stand, I placed my red fabric on it, creating several combinations, focusing on some body elements, such as breasts, hips and shoulder, moving on progressively onto more abstract ideas.

The result left me a bit frustrated, nothing really aroused my interest.

Surely, it was impressive, due to the vivid contrast existing between the stand surface and fabric texture, but the placement and its overall allure, was pretty bulky, heavy and old.

The fact was, it really did not communicate nor mean anything to me, and there was no way to conceal it. My choices behind those unlucky attempts, were not reasoned, nor inspired by a deep sense of understanding of the garment shape to adopt for that specific concept, the direction to pursuit and the message to transmit, it was just offering a physical version of me anxiously working with the obsession of moving on rather than concentrate on what I really wanted to explain with my work.

Anyway, before destroying them, I had the wise idea of taking some pictures, in order to calmly analyse what was wrong and disharmonious within those looks, as well as producing the initial part of my *"primary research"* (conducted and elaborated by myself).

What I was really missing was a sharp reflection on which perspective to embrace, considering the vast and infinite field of possibility I had within the exploration of "maternal bonds".
The thread would have been the main vehicle for sure,

figuring the connection, interaction and disruption of it, but the presence of links and references in terms of garments, was necessary to then build a consistent story.

Remembrances, sometimes can offer a wide range of inputs, dense, nostalgic and definitely evocative, but my internal structure, was still immature to give adequate support to the intense self-discovery creative journey, and to translate coherently all the information at my disposal.

The depth of the concept, as well as its psychological dimension and significant quantity of hidden elements awaken, drove me to a kind of "nervous break-down".

I got stuck.

The silent flood of emotions between the immaculate pages of my sketch-book, and my undisclosed parts, was interrupted.

All of my intimate doors progressively closed, suspending the secret dialogue within my inner voice.

I was unconsciously banning my own channels, due to the hushed sound of the weighty memories I had been stirring up. The only problem was that, the project itself was talking about "my story, my memories, and my inner experience", despite its relation to artworks, so closing the barrier of my discovery phase, would have inevitably affected its result and my creative verve.

I could not stop this story. On the contrary, I should have started to shout it out loud.

As I previously said, art represents a vehicle, a human vehicle, prone to unwrap individual feelings and emotional baggage, establishing strong connections, capable of touching the unreachable persona, its aims and thoughts, hidden within each type of barrier.

And, just how the case was for Louise Bourgeois, my silent

deepest voice had been awaken, just by the view of her vivid, poetic art-works, producing a kind of domino effect in me.
But the questions still remained.

Is it safe to look into our emotional abysses?

What if, after that, they look into our current beings? [16]

How to deal with and manage what is inside our Pandora's box, and once opened, what is it going to happen if its content is dramatically scary, embarrassing and overwhelming?

Are we really ready for a "face to face" with the "persona" hidden within each of us?

Luckily and unluckily, depending on the point of view, creative processes could trigger psychological channels, involving and connecting to their raw elements.
On one level, creative people, are dealing with the same problems as everyone else, such as insecurities, traumas, mood disorder, etc., and as a result some of those problems become magnified by the work artists do, due to their tendency of "butting up" against the issue again and again through their work that deals with it. [17]

According to this thesis "art could be considered as a guaranty of sanity" [18]. *But, at which cost?*

---

[16] Friedrich Nietzsche "Beyond good an evil"

[17] Daniel Grant "Should artists fear therapy" The Observer (on-line page)

[18] Louise Bourgeois

Immersing oneself into a deep, disturbed dimension, even managing the entire process of letting emotional concerns and disorders come out, will undeniably lead the individual to a constrictive dimension of suffering, which might be compared to a moment of "insanity".

The flood of suppressed feelings, definitely influences and channels the imaginative process, providing a sense of fulfilment and satisfaction within the artist, while paradoxically operating on a negative level, overwhelming psychologically the individual, with a considerable, metaphorical weight.

This phenomenology, often considered as an effective way of tackling problems, moves on a circular basis, creating a loop, in which antithetical emotional statuses alternate, without really offering an adequate cure.

So art is, sometimes a "guaranty of sanity at the price of insanity", with relevant and beneficial effects that might occur, such as a new sense of awareness, a mature and conscious self-knowledge, as well as a progressive internal evolution.

In line with it, I may have not found any solution, any rest, any peace, interrupting the flow, blocking the process and suffocating myself. I had passed the line, already, moving too many steps in my "emotional ground", the only option was proceeding along the route.

Observing the pictures taken, showing a variety of options, I realized that, I should have paid more attention, not only to the red threads, but also to a strong and meaningful garment construction, drenched of evocative power.

The initial stand-works, showed their lacks in terms of sophistication, along with a partial sense of confusion during the textile placement.

Everything seemed messy, heavy and carelessly combined. The initial looks were almost unusable, so I had to opt for a different approach, employing this time various media, mixing and matching existing garments, which could have provided a rough idea in terms of shape, to then conduct on more experimentations.

I was conscious of the miserable results obtained, and I reasonably felt mopey. There was this flourishing magma of emotions, undisclosed in me, unexpressed, delicately surfacing my thoughts, and even so, I could not find my way to give it coherency and consistency.

It was so frustrating.

The concept seemed interesting, the connections well reasoned, so...

What was really going wrong?

Creative processes generally follow a kind of "scheme", even though the common understanding of "creative" would tend to make people think otherwise.

The imaginative dimension is often confused with a "surreal world" with no order inside, in which raw and fine elements move in unknown and inexplicable ways; but this is partially true.

To an extent, creative processes differ from person to person, operating on a deep emotional level that happen to be different and unpredictable for each individual; but, while the main background, heritage and perception capacity might vary, the crucial role of giving ideas a "structure" is still necessary, no matter how a creative process starts.

Artistic projects need a pattern behind, a guideline, they are not merely a "short- time enlightenment", otherwise it would be almost impossible to give a sense of meaningful wholeness to the final outcome.

Thoughts, beliefs, notions and ideas, urge to be defined, organised, prioritised and then processed, such as it happens within a story.

It is vital to create an introduction, a corpus and then, a conclusion, missing some of the steps may lead to inconclusive, disconnected and poor results.

Set aside my beloved red textile, I oriented my attention and energy to garment research, carefully selecting, this time, proportions, volumes and materials that matched my purpose.

I opted for a kind of "cocoon" shape, and outwear appearances, aligned to my childish memories. These type of clothes were basically democratic, neutral, with clean lines, capable of reconstituting a lost sense of protection, of urgency to be seen for what is inside, and feel safe in it. The fit needed to be exaggerated, the silhouette distorted, evoking a typical behaviour children have when using parents garments.

The project acquired immediately melancholic nuances, swaying between the oneiric and memories ground.

I was envisioning these wacky figure, carrying on, fluctuating clothes, suspended on threads, made as a result of a perfect fusion between an "outer shell" (outwear), and delicate shirts all deconstructed and reconstructed in a disturbing order.

I moved back to the stand, starting the real draping process, cutting garments into pieces and reassembling them.

I studied key details, altering, enlarging and reducing several parts, and finally I took some pictures to stick into my sketch-book, ready for the "design development".

Despite the intellectual, reasoned approach, the results was still a bit flat, the garment used showed a too literal interpretation, while other concerns were still waiting to be

addressed. The first issue was how to reconnect and visually allocate the threads on this new cocoon shape, and then how to manipulate the clothes ideas in order to have a more complex and sophisticated result.

In that occasion, an objective impossibility compromised the progression of my exploration, despite the considerable quantity of clothes bought, once cut all of them, I remained empty-handed, and I had to find out a trick to progress with the garment design and experimentation.

The idea of using magazines, collages etc. became vital for me to solve at least one of the problems I was facing.

I selected all of the most attractive images of outwear, collecting diverse styles and shapes, then I followed the "well-known procedure" of attaching my pieces of paper on an inspiring basis.

I worked on these illustrations for a couple of days, secretly waiting for the start of the tutorials, at the end of the week.

At the point reached, I really needed a honest and tough suggestion, considering that I had been working alone for approximately one month.

Before the due date, I checked all of my work, organizing it nicely and professionally, to then lay it out on the desk; threads were accurately placed on the left hand side, my draping attempts printed and halved piled and clipped, my garment experimentations pinned on the stand, everything seemed to be consciously prepared and displayed.

I was ready.

My corner was a genuine combination of good results

(opinions are my own), doubts (things I was concerned about) and failures (such as the messy, gross thread draping).

Tutorial day

Tutors were impressed by the quantity of work showed all over the room, we all did a nice job!

Then, when it was my turn, we started an interesting discussion about the reasons of the choices operated, meaning of the concept, purposes behind etc.

Secretly embarrassed by my incomplete project (during my working experience I used to ONLY show final results to my boss), I kept on explaining my creative perspectives and aims, noticing, out of my expectation, a sign of pleasant approval for the sharp decision of displaying every steps, every failing attempts without concerns.

It resulted to be extremely important for them to have a

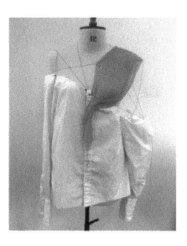

Draping attempt with thin, waxed cotton threads.

look and deep understanding of my personal methodology, so that they used to consider far more appealing the entire creative process rather than a banal, sterile outcome.

The failing options, became at some point, centre stage, and sadly, the massive red textile, convulsively arranged, had to LEAVE.

What a tragedy!

The way I had been conducting my design development, unfortunately did not contemplate any attractive possibility in which to include it, and although I was deeply supporting their thesis, some concerns on the idea of putting aside "my creation" still remained.

That night I tried so bad to incorporate my threads, doing hundreds of draping.

After the 99th attempt, despondent, tired and discouraged, I finally took away all the delicate textile which was connecting the shirt shoulder to a detached sleeve, leaving absent-mindedly a fine little thread in that position... and the magic happened!

I had an incredulous look to the stand, It was completely different..acquiring a strong attitude,without the heaviness of that red colour spot.

The dramatic event, then turned into a pivotal point for my project.

Everything came full circle, the heaviness of the oversize garment, gently held by this fragile fine thread, this sense of interruption, of uncertainty and vulnerability, that individuals unconsciously experienced in their lives.

The unexpected look made the point, summarising at its best, my purpose and aims. The red thread turned into a metaphor of our existence, and so needed to be tiny and thin, with different length, strongly anchored on the shoulder, the body area in which emotions feelings and pain generally concentrate.

It should have offered a vivid contrast between its precarious condition (due to the fragile nature), and the clumsiness of clothes, filled and imbued with human needs and necessities, often incompatible with their inner-being.

My idea was to give a prominent role to the threads, leaving the space all around, such as background, garments in neutral tone, apart for the almost subtle red line.

I imagined the collection all white, except for a pink trench, as a memento of my childhood, a warm spot in this vast expanse of white memories.

While developing the clothes, I started to think on how to properly and effectively present my project, while the option of using some models did not produce any interest, nor excitement, in me.

It appeared banal, and basically not suitable.

I was looking for some solutions which could have supported my ideas and concept in their wholeness, summing up the story, in a way.

Although, as a designer, I was expected to make decisions always referring to some kind of "fashion schemes", enhancing garments wearabilty, consequent look and appearance on a human figure, which was in a way the core itself of "making fashion", concerning my project, I felt unusually more interested in its sense and meaning, so that I decided to pursuit an evocative perspective and approach rather than sticking to clothes literal function and use. I was still determined to "do fashion", but in that case, I wanted my collection to be

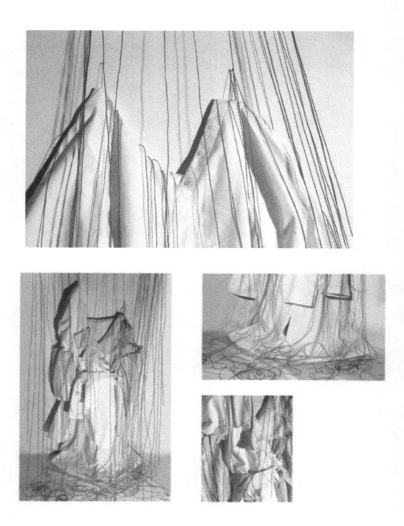

"Installation trial": Each garment would have been placed at different positions and heights, suspended on thin waxed cotton threads, allowing a sense of becoming and living to the scenery itself; as it is the case with human thoughts that incessantly dance, a sort of interactive space of "floating, living memories, white soul that wave propelled by their existence".

the main focus, something to look at, something to reflect on, and question about, not merely something cute or attractive to wear.

Nor stands or models would have been employed for the final presentation, shirts and coat would have been hung on the ceiling with metres of threads spread all over the floor.

My purpose was to recreate a kind of installation of a soft oneiric space, an empty room, plenty of natural light. Unfortunately, I did not have the opportunity of exploring this hypothetical solution, nor the space to do so. The final presentation, that also matched the day of the internal interview for the craved post grad, took place in the current building and rooms, so there was a physical impossibility in practical and social terms.

We were six, and for each of us a predefined area to allocate our works and experimentations had been assigned; according to this, I managed to use my rectangular desk, taking advantage of the ceiling and walls, hanging my pieces on a vertical dimension, leaving the work-station for my sketch-book and portfolio.

The final, raw attempt of "installing" my project, resulted in an unusual spot, the hung shirt adorned with tonnes of threads that were falling down as a waterfall, caught immediately the eyes of the viewer, even if was not resembling the neutral space with floating memories I had aimed for.

After all, there is a right time for everything, and probably in that specific circumstance I was not properly ready to step outside the canonical fashion world.

The day arrived, and, my red spot, did the work.

It gained the desired interest and positive feedback, while

several new suggestions and recommendations on how to progress with my knowledge and creative growth, did not fail to come.

I added a pinch more confidence within myself and my capabilities, and definitely crowned my dream...

I got a place at the Post-Grad...

I was in!!

Working on this project, I opened up my channels, the most intimate ones, disclosing silent obsession of using stories as a starting point for my creative journey.

According to the importance of being honest towards the "self imaginative discovery", I genuinely faced key elements capable to trigger my emotional ground, and I have immersed myself without regrets.

I learnt that art, has a powerful, overwhelming influence on me, probably more than I could have ever expected, and above all, I understood the urgency of internalising and giving voice to topics and social, anthropological issues, which are in a way deeply connected to my inner being; I could not suffocate this tendency, on the contrary I appreciate it, and massively exploit it in my creative process.

My curiosity, growing up, while adopting different shades and nuances, pushed me during this journey, to continuously question my condition as a "human", driving me to the ultimate conclusion that I really need to talk, explain, engage and discuss, giving rise to doubts, reflections, ideas and reactions.

I believe in the power of communicating, and sharing.

I believe in story-telling.

I want to feel people's emotional, authentic engagement and participation.

I would love to be a story-teller; no matter if it is through fashion, art, garment writing or installation.

I believe in the power of words, of honesty and authenticity, we really need more of these, and more "story-telling" in our era, especially in fashion.

On a more intellectually involved dimension, garments and arts in general should be committed to express a point of view, to celebrate a designer's unique DNA, talking about their roots, heritage, story and experiences, while playing a role in terms of awareness raising and positive mark to leave.

Nowadays the focus and attention are progressively moving onto deeper aspects, and so I want to do, by favouring "the meaning rather than the shape, the process rather than the commercial needs, the hidden core of things".

I strongly support the idea that every object, or human product, or art work, and so on, needs a story, a behind the scene, in order to reconnect with an ancestral meaningful dimension, in which individuals can feel part of something, rather than forcefully alienated .

The shiny, sparkly world of plastic, perfection, strict commercial logic and preconceived ideals, we are deeply imbued in, needs to be replaced by a sense of realness, vividness that could talk about "people", leaving even if for a second the spectacular trend of the contemporary era.

The urgency of "finding a place for sanity", while working on my project, revealed the thoughts, necessities and aims both as a creative person and as an individual, a perpetual condition of "in-becoming", that largely reflected in the project itself, making it a kind of "open-canvass" in progressive movement.

I am not sure I could and would ever put a " full-stop"to my "living memories" project, according to the will behind it and its inner meaning and nature.

Potentially, there will always be an open possibility or option to approach it once again, with, each time , different perspectives. Its evocative, meaningful power, could give rise to a fervent new pleasure, of conducting new exploration, new experimentations and techniques of the same concept, which is in a way kind of summing up my emotional ground.

There is a time in our life, we might have to deal with the idea that we can look at our things, ourselves, noticing and accepting their/our beauty even in the capacity of being unfinished, as an open-window, breathing a sense of wholeness in the constant condition of "in becoming".

In a way, the thread project, contained and revealed my status, of a book partially written, with lots of empty, hopefully flourishing pages that craved to be filled.

An incredible amount of possibilities, of layering, an infinite potential still waiting to be exposed and explained.

At the beginning of my journey, my creative exploration, I was looking for my raw persona, my inner self, and probably I still am , with a bit more awareness and consciousness by my side.

After all, life is a "never ending learning process", with the magnificent, deliberate choice of pushing our horizons trough curiosity, or just conveniently sleeping in our comfort zones, enabling us to create several hypothetical combinations, we can either choose and expect or simply face along the way.

This is what I would like to consider a time,"our time of possibilities, immense and intimate".

Have you guys found yours, yet?

Acknowledgements

I wish to offer my heartfelt thanks to Professor and Editor Ruth Finnegan, who believed in my potential and capabilities, since the very beginning, giving me the amazing opportunity of challenging myself, writing my story. Her warm support, and bright suggestions, meant so much, helping me to progress even when I felt emotionally lost.

Thank you Ruth.

I would also thank Mirko, my partner, my friend, my everything, who assisted me, day by day, during this journey, thrilling my creativity, discussing my doubts, always showing his sincere commitment and genuine help, and providing the best pen supply ever.

Thank you my love.

This book has been my first, real experience of writing, and I could not be more grateful for the possibility had, and for the vibrant energy the amazing people in my life gave me, contributing with their uniqueness to cheer me up at any stage of my creative process, and put up with me during my disruptive moments of discouragement.

Thank you Dad, for your calm and reassuring approach.

Thanks to my colleagues, for their sharp advices and inspiring conversations.

Thanks to my family and best friends, to remind me the way.

Thanks to my Tutors for helping me to let my inner voice surface, for pushing my limits and beliefs, and for having made me determined enough to cope with good and bad critics.

MARELLA CAMPAGNA

Thanks to my grandfather and to my mother who, even if they are no longer physically and earthly by my side, taught me to believe in myself, the importance of being curious, of learning, and above all that "Hard work beats talent, when talent does not work".

164

Bibliography

Amabile, Teresa, (1998) "How to kill creativity", Harvard Business Review, https://hbr.org/1998/09/how-to-kill-creativity

Bohm, David, (1998) "On Creativity"

Bourgeois, Louise, (2012) "The return of the repressed", Psychoanalytical writings

Calderin, Jay, (2011) "Fashion Design Essentials"

Fuchs, Lisa, (2014) "The role of fast failure in driving innovation", http://researchaccess.com/2014/04/fast-failure/

Grant, Daniel, (2017) "Should artists fear therapy" The Observer, https://observer.com/2017/02/why-do-artists-fear-psychotherapy/

Kleon, Austin , (2014) "SHOW YOUR WORK!: 10 ways to share your creativity and get discovered"

Mc Dowell, Patrick, (2018) "1 Granary", Instagram Page

Nietzsche, Friedrich, (1886)"Beyond good an evil"

Patterson, Ransom, (2015) " Want to think better? Avoid these six cognitive bias", https://collegeinfogeek.com/avoid-cognitive-biases/

Questions for discussion

1. What do you think of the style of the book, alternating narrative parts with more general and complex reflections? Does it help and intrigue your understanding and interest?

2. What do you think about the illustrations in general? What about the pictures showing "failing attempts" and "in-becoming processes"? Is it useful for you to see more "behind the scene", rather than final outcomes? Why?

3. Do you find it easy to visually connect and understand the illustrations of my "Thread project" and the creative aims and purposes explained, behind it? Looking at them, what impression do you have? What interpretation would you give?

4. Have you ever experienced problems in facing the "failure"? Have you ever felt blocked due to this reason?

5. Do you agree with the importance of being curious, open and continuously learning? Why?

6. How was your view of fashion, before reading this book? Has it changed? Does the book provide or add something useful in terms of insights and clarifications about what fashion is about?

7. What do you think about the "creative process"? Is it helpful to have a view from the inside? Do you have any concerns about how it has been explained and treated?

8. Do you believe in the power of sharing, and communicating? Do you think our society, schools, Universities etc. help us in doing so? What about social media? Are they contributing to this process?

9. What do you think about the existing bond between

our inner self and things we love? Do you think that a job could help us to grow and progress towards a self-discovery process? Have you ever experienced it?

10. What do you do when you feel stuck or scared? Is it related to performance anxiety?

11. What are your beliefs, concerning the "preconceived ideals of beauty and perfection" promoted nowadays, in regard to our aesthetics and own performance? Would you prefer to conform to it rather than "be the difference"? Do you think we need more authenticity or more perfection?

12. What is your point of view about rules and strict teaching approaches? Have you ever experienced a situation of partial or complete autonomy within a task development? And if so, what reactions and results did you have? Was it fruitful?

13. Have you enjoyed the reading? Do you have any suggestions for me? Things to ask?

I have always dreamt about the possibility of contacting an author to ask, discuss and question topics or to simply connect with them and figure out what was in their mind.

You can do this, our technology allows us to stay in touch and have a talk, even if we are miles apart, so please I will be very happy to engage and discover all of your impressions and thoughts.

Let me know, if you like, at marella.campagna@icloud.com or visit my facebook (@MarellaCampagnaGrimaldi) and instagram page: (@marellacampagna).

Reading suggestions

Dear reader...

Thank you for reaching here! I hope that you enjoyed the story.

If you liked it, why not look for some insights concerning the topic discussed?

Here you can find some suggestions of readings, magazines and Instagram pages to look at.

Readings about creative process, fashion, art and mental tips to stay at your best:

- Teresa Amabile, "How to kill creativity", on Harward business review
- Austin Kleon, author of several, interesting, thrilling books, I personally suggest "Steal like an artist" and "SHOW YOUR WORK!: 10 ways to share your creativity and get discovered"
- David Bohm, Emeritus professor of physics, widely know for his significant contribution to the discussion on the relationship between art and science. Complex book, but really enlightening, " On creativity"
- Bonnie Marranca and Gautam Dasgupta, "Conversation on art and performance"
- Ransom Patterson, "Want to think better? Avoid 6 cognitive bias", College Info Geek web page
- Louise Bourgeois, "The return of the repressed"
- Jon K. Show and Theo Reeves-Evison, "Fiction as method"
- Ursula K. Le Guin, "Steering the craft"

- Mads Nygaard Folkman, "The aesthetics of imagination in design"
- Jay Calderin, "Fashion design essential"
- Isabella Dothel, "Fashion: Box"

Some Fashion magazines:
- 1 Granary
- Another Magazine
- I-D
- Love
- Dazed & Confused
- Hunger

Some Instagram pages:
- royalacademyarts
- bafcsm
- fashionfoliocsm
- bof
- oneofa___kind
- 1granary
- toiletpapermagazine
- tate
- thelovemagazine
- designmuseum
- fashion-east
- selfservicemagazine
- 1granary-showroom
- parsonsfashionmfa
- #trendforecast
- marellacampagna

Hearing Others' Voices

Hearing Others' Voices: A transcultural and transdisciplinary book series in simple and straightforward language, to inform and engage general readers, undergraduates and, above all, sixth formers in recent advances in thought, unaccountably overlooked areas of the world, and key issues of the day.

Lightning Source UK Ltd.
Milton Keynes UK
UKHW020835290519
343516UK00002B/5/P